The British Dissonance

A. Kingsley Weatherhead

The British Dissonance

Essays on Ten
Contemporary Poets

University of Missouri Press
Columbia & London, 1983

Library of Congress Cataloging in Publication Data
Weatherhead, A. Kingsley (Andrew Kingsley), 1923–
The British dissonance.
Includes bibliographical references and index.
1. English poetry—20th century—History and
criticism.   I. Title.
PR611.W4 1983   821'.914'09   82–13559
ISBN 0–8262–0391–4

For permissions, see pp. 237–38.

For Lyn Kristin
and Svein Atle
with love

Contents

Tom Raworth; photograph by Rob Rusk

Lee Harwood; photograph courtesy of Lee Harwood

Charles Tomlinson; photograph by Judith Aronson

Ted Hughes; photograph by Layle Silbert

Roy Fisher; photograph by Joanna Voit, courtesy of Judy Daish Associates

Geoffrey Hill; photograph courtesy of Andre Deutsch Ltd.

David Jones; photograph courtesy of University of Wales
Press on behalf of the Welsh Arts Council

Anselm Hollo; photograph by David Abrams

Basil Bunting; photograph courtesy of Popperfoto

1

Introduction

The poets discussed in the following chapters are included in a recent anthology bent on demonstrating that, contrary to broad rumor, there is in fact a new British poetry, one that is developing the art even as American poetry is.[1] The editor includes a few older figures whose work has been neglected; he includes no women poets. From the poets represented in this anthology I have selected those who make the more interesting departures from traditional verse forms. Many of them have substituted for the sound effects of such forms a dissonance, reflecting uncertainty about the old closed poetry. But the *dissonance* of the title refers also, metaphorically, to the sense, ubiquitous among these poets, that the order poetry imposes on reality is alien to it. *Dissonance* will be remembered as one of the key words in Williams's *Paterson*; and it is to be noted that most of the poets here have been influenced by modern American poetry. An American scholar has declared that the postwar period ushered in a new divergence between American and British poetry,[2] and the quotations she marshals from individual contemporary poets are persuasive. One might safely generalize in addition that the British have been slower than the Americans to break out of the old, conventional, formal restraints. Americans at least have thought so, both in contemporary painting and

1

in poetry: "Stop sipping your afternoon tea, *belch* if you need to," Denise Levertov instructed Charles Tomlinson,[3] exercising the liberation procured her by her translation to America and her liberation from the confinement of conventional form. (Tomlinson, who lacks the talent for this or other kinds of exhibitionism, is civilized, is not Walt Whitman, and never omits to close a parenthesis.)

It would be a mistake, however, to make too much of the differences between the two poetries: the Atlantic has shrunk to a creek in the Global Village, anyway, and for some years the English-speaking peoples have been amazed, baffled, or outraged by the same encroaching phenomena and their intellects engaged by many of the same ideas. And most of the novelties of contemporary Britain have for some time had currency in America.

The poets discussed in the following pages suggest that the two poetries have, in fact, a good deal in common, not least because of the strong American influence, appearing sometimes as a passing exercise but sometimes integrated into a poet's mature style. Both T. S. Eliot and Ezra Pound influenced David Jones, for instance; Pound influenced Basil Bunting and Matthew Mead; William Carlos Williams, Wallace Stevens, Marianne Moore, and Robert Lowell are all detectable in the earlier poems of Charles Tomlinson; Robert Lowell influenced Geoffrey Hill; Frank O'Hara influenced Lee Harwood; and Charles Olson influenced Anselm Hollo, Lee Harwood, and Tom Raworth via Ed Dorn, with whom Raworth studied at Essex. There are also American influences that are less progressive than these, such as those of Allen Tate and John Crowe Ransom on Geoffrey Hill and of Richard Wilbur and Ransom on Ted Hughes. Some of the relationships between the poetries are pleasantly entangled: Richard Wilbur, the American, writes like W. H. Auden, who wrote in part like Marianne

Moore; Ted Hughes, the Englishman, acknowledges his debt to Wilbur.

"All we can do," Thomas Hardy told Robert Graves, "is to write on the old themes in the old styles, but try to do a little better than those who went before us." He thought free verse would come to nothing. He would hardly have allowed that poetry without external form might have structure, still less that poetry without structure might be poetry. The conversation with Graves was early in the 1920s—when in America Williams was writing the innovative poems of *Spring and All*. Hardy's was a reactionary pronouncement, no doubt; but there is nothing in Graves's poetry to discountenance it, and there were critics in the 1950s who considered the departures of the Pound-Eliot revolution not a development in the main line of the history of poetry but a huge excursion from which the art would duly return. It did in fact return in the fifties with poets of the Movement, who, though they promoted a number of negative principles of their own, tended to stick to the old styles and conspired, says Donald Davie, "to pretend that Eliot and Pound never happened."[4] And Graves who had talked with Hardy was still around, *punctum indifferens*, undiverted by modish change. Among the Movement poets, Philip Larkin has followed close to Hardy in both practice and precept. Thom Gunn, in his early work at least, was traditional: he was trained at Stanford by Yvor Winters, his respect for whom led him to invest in the rational statement of understood experience. All the same, in the last two or three decades, there has been first a growing contempt for the old styles and later a massive reaction against them.

Poets of the generation following the Movement writers (a generation in these swift times being about five years) reproved their predecessors for the old style. Hughes charged them with having confined themselves to "the cosiest arrangement of society" and having avoided the horrors that were rife in man's broadest experiences of the world.[5] The latent terror that Larkin discovers in apparently the cosiest arrangements would, one might have thought, be enough for anybody, but the terrors he faces up to are ugliness, boredom, spiritual numbness, and despair rather than whatever forms of active bestiality are proffered from outside. His terrors, moreover, are held beneath the surface and conveyed, albeit powerfully, generally by hints or implications only, and generally in rhetoric, whereas the external violence others record comes to us in images. Movement poetry, in fact, occasioned some amazement for the mask of bland urbanity it assumed in order to neglect to face recent monstrosities—the Nazi death camps, in particular, and all the violence and cruelty for which they stand as the ultimate symbol; Vietnam and the other horrors rationally fabricated in this century; and the colossal political turbulence of our world.

To one critic, the reticence of the Movement seemed a flight into Georgian poetry, and his criticism is reminiscent of that which the Georgians encountered: Movement poetry was "a return to a personal well-ordered and fairly decent version of reality which denied the violence and the horror of the war which immediately preceded it." Indeed, "however accomplished" the work of Movement poets is, "their conception of man was severely diminished, the area of life, on which they established themselves so confidently, severely restricted. Those appalling images of mass horror that the war had released to communal consciousness . . . hardly involved them, for the rational, ordered consciousness and traditional decencies could not contain or comprehend irrationality on this scale; the unloosing of the blood-dimmed tide, the anarchy that Yeats predicted, found poetry vaguely incredulous and totally unprepared."[6] To which it might, of course, be added that Yeats was not *predicting* the blood-dimmed tide; he was recording it, and he was doing so in verse submissive to traditional exterior controls.

Today's most remarkable departures from tradition are made with the intention of preventing the domination of poetic forms. Many poets, many writers in general, believe that words distort experience, especially words in formal, traditional patterns. "The Word," for Henri Chopin, one of its miscellaneous detractors, "has permitted life to lie."[7] Laura Riding's recent message is that art cheats truth, the poetic art most of all.[8] Urbanity is discredited. "The radical character, the 'violence' of this reconstruction in contemporary art," says Herbert Marcuse, "seems to indicate that it does not rebel against one style or another but against 'style' itself, against the art-form of art, against the traditional 'meaning' of art."[9] Ted Hughes, after his brilliant mastery of traditional poetic language and techniques in his earliest volumes, jettisoned the heritage: he felt that nicely turned verse or verse in a tradition created a barrier before reality and that it had no place in a real world of violence—a world where a poet may crouch in a doorway while bullets lift the cobblestones out of the street.[10] So he responded first in the "super-ugly" language of *Crow* and then in the coined language of *Orghast*, invented and hence virginal of earlier use and connotation, "purged of the haphazard associations of English, which continually tries to supplant experience and truth with the mechanisms of its own autonomous life."[11]

Poets like Charles Tomlinson who still use traditional forms are inclined to speak of the *discovery* of order. Those writers, on the other hand, who spurn form speak of it disparagingly and without question as an imposition precluding sincerity and truth and distinguish their own work as Keats distinguished his from the product of the "Wordsworthian or egotistical sublime."[12] In his own way, however, Tomlinson is concerned with the distortion that is suffered by reality in art form: although he characteristically presents images of frozen motion, he knows that reality, in fact, is flux and cannot be contained. Roy Fisher, much more wary, believes the poet's creative act is itself an infliction and, in his poem *City*, asserts that he should absent himself from his city for fear of endowing it with a structure. Matthew Mead gathers incongruous fragments of experience in a sequence, a medium that M. L. Rosenthal calls "the outstanding formal development in our poetry for over a century," having "evolved out of a serious need for an encompassing poetry, one really involved with what our lives mean."[13] David Jones, in *The Anathémata*— the earliest poem considered below—assembles what are advisedly fragments, tying them to the Mass, but so loosely that he admittedly leaves room for "meanderings."[14] Lee Harwood avoids fixed, final statements or relegates them, by use of quotation marks, to the status of a curiosity. He declares that the poem made of fragments rather than the structured one is close to the world. Tom Raworth's poems, often assemblages, are formed by intuition rather than by intelligence. The poets' intentions or those attributed to them may be some distance away from the respective executions: poems "involved with what our lives mean" and poems "close to the world" suggest mimesis. Some of the poetic works discussed below are univocal—mimetic in the old sense. Others (including Harwood's) may present an illusion of reality but then pointedly destroy it or maintain it only inconsistently as the poem moves out of its frame into the reader's living space. In contemporary literature, reference is only one of the uses of language, and it may appear among the works discussed below, as elsewhere, as "a possession and an instrument for accomplishing certain tasks."[15]

Most of these and many other contemporary poets avoid the familiar techniques that have traditionally supplied structure: a logical or narrative sequence, or repetition—rhythm and rhyme, stanzas, the reflection of the elements of the theme in varied forms, the repetition of an image or of one feature of an image in another, the reflection of the ideas in symbol or in the shape of the framework—the features, in a word, that for centuries have supported the reader. Often a contemporary poet deliberately seeks to withhold the satisfaction that structure was wont to supply; he may seek, indeed, in the words of Roy Fisher, a "dislocative effect."[16] The literary atmosphere is heady in its suspicion of the symmetry and the elegance of traditional structures, once desiderata that now apparently appeal only to scientists, as two biologists on the brink of the DNA discovery tell each other over lunch that a structure as aesthetically satisfying as the one they had hypothesized must perforce be right,[17] assuming that beauty is truth, truth beauty, a proposition somewhat neglected in the contemporary artistic culture.

Of the poets discussed below, Geoffrey Hill exerts the most control over his verse, and, more than any others, he knows how he wishes to be read. In this respect he is unlike Basil Bunting or Tom Raworth, who both leave much up to the reader, or Lee Harwood, who regards a poem as complete only when it is being read. Bunting's work aspires to the condition of music, though he has also compared a work of art to a bowl, a thing constructed, and "the attempt to find any meaning in it would be manifestly absurd." Harwood has also spoken of the poem as an object—"an object made by the writer that he gives to the reader." But he also calls on the reader to complement the poems, as if filling in the missing half of a torn telegram.[18]

With Tom Raworth's poems, constituted largely of pieces of ordinary experience lacking any particular significance, the problem is less a matter of understanding than one of responding with the senses. He is instructing us that this is our world; we should see it in the way Claes Oldenburg wishes to see, wishing to become an ignorant man again and see the world again with an ignorant eye, trying to "eliminate knowing . . . to forget the name of the thing or what it may be used for."[19] But it is not easy thus to dope the intellect, a difficulty expressed clearly by Alfred North Whitehead.

> We look up and see a coloured shape in front of us and we say—there is a chair. But what we have seen is the mere coloured shape. *Perhaps an artist might not have jumped to the notion of a chair. He might have stopped at the mere contemplation of a beautiful colour and a beautiful shape.* But those of us who are not artists are very prone, especially if we are tired, to pass straight from the perception of the coloured shape to the enjoyment of the chair, in some way of use, or of emotion, or of thought. . . . my friend the artist, who kept himself to the contemplation of colour, shape, and position, was a very highly trained man, and had acquired this facility of ignoring the chair at the cost of great labour.[20]

Recently, both writers and artists in increasing number have proposed as their proper function to wake us up, in the words of John Cage, "to the very life we're living."[21] And the declaration of Victor Shklovsky of over half a century ago comes to us as if it breathed contemporary air: "In order to restore to us the sensation of life, to make us feel things, to make the stone stony, there exists that which we call Art. The purpose of art is to impart to us the sensation of an object as it is *perceived* and not merely as it is *recognized*. . . . the process of perception is an end in itself."[22]

In the aim to enhance the perceptions of their publics, poets and painters come together, and it is noticeable that many contemporary poets are interested in or even associated with the graphic arts. Fisher's work springs from his experience with French surrealist paintings; Raworth has had bound with his work the graphics of Jim Dine; Harwood marks the sections of a book with photographs of warships; Hughes writes poems to the drawings of Leonard Baskin; Tomlinson and David Jones are graphic artists themselves. Concrete poets, such as Ian Hamilton Finlay, have, of course, broken down the barrier between the two media, liberating words from linear order and from their meanings. It is thereby possible that a piece of graphic work, Richard Hamilton's *$he*, for example, or Robert Indiana's *USA 666* or James Rosenquist's *F-111*, may *say* more than a poem.

This book, though, is a series of essays about poetry and the relation of various poets' works to traditional forms. The first essay is a discussion of Charles Tomlinson's poems, which, although largely in formal structures and showing a less radical departure than those of others, manifest consciousness of the distortion exerted by the poetic act.

2

Charles Tomlinson

Tomlinson's poetry does not—not so far, at any rate—manifest any of the more striking departures from the traditions of modernist English and American poetry; it has not, for example, evolved into open form, though it includes occasional prose passages; but it constantly raises the questions, implicitly and explicitly, Is form in reality? Is form in a scene part of the act of perception? Or does form belong not to reality but to the alien order of discourse? In a word, in the literary act is form discovered or imposed? The questions usually receive ambivalent answers. But Tomlinson's manipulation of geometric lines in his poetry and in his substantial body of graphic work is interesting to consider, if it is true, as Wilhelm Worringer suggested, that, by momentarily arresting the flux of being, geometrical regularity in art offers repose to the man disquieted by the obscurity and confusion of the world.[1]

Charles Tomlinson (b. 1927) has received degrees from Cambridge and the University of London. Currently, Tomlinson holds a personal chair in English literature at the University of Bristol. He has taught and lectured in the United States on several occasions. Also a graphic artist, he has had numerous public exhibitions. As a scholar and critic, Tomlinson has contributed to such journals as *Essays in Criticism, Hudson Review, Poetry* (Chicago), *Sewanee Review,* and *TLS*. He has received several honors for his work including honorary degrees from the University of Keele and Colgate University. He was also made Honorary Fellow of Queen's College, Cambridge. In 1975, Tomlinson was named a Fellow of the Royal Society of Literature.

Tomlinson has amassed by now a substantial number of volumes of poetry, his own and translations. They contain no lines that spring or will spring to the mind to appease it in specific situations—the criterion Auden once proposed for testing; for of the clothes of the perfectly dressed man one remembers nothing. The poems are formed, one must imagine, with exquisite care and they are exquisite. Tomlinson is admired by traditionalists, obviously, but he is accepted also by the radicals—those in whose presence one must not praise Philip Larkin.

He bridges, in fact, a number of divisions. He is from Staffordshire, the country of Arnold Bennett's fiction, territory subjugated to pottery, sprouting the monstrous bottle kilns that are imaged on the cover of one of his volumes, *A Peopled Landscape*, and honored in his memory. Not consigning his memories conventionally into the scene of frustration, he returns to his old territories and can express horror at the remodeling of the old performed according to the values of suburbia, finding some beauty in the "comforting brick," and writing to "rescue" the area.[2] He moved away from a working-class source, bringing with him a scarcely detectable Midland accent, detected, however, and deplored by Percy Lubbock, to whom he had been hired to read.[3] His achievement in both poetry and criticism gives the lie to the theory that holds the two incompatible—doing and teaching, in Bernard Shaw's unkind dichotomy. Particularly in a period when American influence on all the English arts and on its culture in general has grown beyond any previous dimensions, Tomlinson must be recognized as one of the first to have bridged the gap between English and American poetry; like some of his British colleagues, he has made significant importations.

In the fifties and sixties, along with Gael Turnbull, he promoted recent American exports in modern poetry in England. He was somewhat solitary in his efforts in days when, for example, no local publisher had brought out a collection of William Carlos Williams, whose aural effects William Empson had declared to be inaudible to the British ear. They were not inaudible to Tomlinson, however, who received congratulations from Williams on his sensitivity to the American idiom, a sensitivity manifest in a poem written under Williams's guidance.[4] As a critic, among a good deal of work on European and British poets, including an edition of the poems of Octavio Paz, Tomlinson has edited the Marianne Moore volume in the Twentieth Century Series in America and the Penguin collection on Williams in England.

In his own poetry, as will appear, the presence of Wallace Stevens is audible. He can write like Robert Lowell occasionally, delivering out of his hat, for example, the sudden concrete curiosity among abstractions or among images only remotely associated, coming on in Lowell's old familiar enjambment:

> Hard edges of the houses press
>> On the after-music senses, and refuse to burn,
> Where an ice-cream van circulates the estate
>> Playing Greensleeves.[5]

Or

>> "Duck!" you cried, George,
> The day the militia filed out with rifles
> At a Shriner celebration, but that was the pastoral era
>> Of sixty-six.[6]

He has also caught the cadences of Marianne Moore, her characteristically unbalanced compound sentence, for example, in "Ship's Waiters," a poem in Williams's triadic line, dedicated to Marianne Moore:

> Nothing
>> can diminish
>>> that peculiar concert

of either the gliding
   man, or the infallible
      freaked quadruped, but one
can equal it.[7]

Or he may use the integrated quotation as Moore does:

Mayakovsky
has it!—
   "in the place
of style, an austere
   disposition of bolts."[8]

Then, like so many of his American contemporaries, Tomlinson shows over and over again the importance of the example of Williams: the clean and clear observation like that of the red wheel barrow,

Between
slats of the garden
bench, and strung
to their undersides
ride clinging
rain-drops,[9]

or the effort, slight as it is, to overcome the domination of chronological time—

they wait, sitting
(the moment)
on the earth floor
(is expansible)
saying very little.[10]

He has gone so far with American poetry and with Williams; but of later developments in form, he has not partaken. His efforts to counter chronological order are minimal; poems remain in their frames and are not noticeably concrete, immediate, or particular; they come to their endings; they do not repudiate syntax or avoid orders that are claimed to belong properly only to discourse.

13

While his poetry does not depart radically from the tradition, however, his attitude to chance implies a species of openness: "The fact that 'chance' rhymes with 'dance,'" he says, "is a nutrifying thought for the artist, whether he is poet or painter."[11] And in a poem called "The White Van," "chance / unblinds certitude."[12]

But chance operates in the paintings, where brushed and blotted symmetries produce trees, waves, and stones. The pictures *Landscape with Bathers* and, to only a slightly smaller extent, *Willendorf Grotto* show a reliance on non-images,[13] a kind of openness that parallels the reliance of many contemporary poets on passages of silence, used to make a statement that is uncontrolled by the limitation words necessarily exert. Tomlinson does not use silence in his poems but achieves his success by accepting limits and working for his effects within them. In the graphics, on the other hand, he relinquishes the controls that he maintains in the poems: he is willing to leave space unprogrammed and undesignated. The title *Willendorf Grotto* suggests Venus, and there are a number of uberous shapes to justify it. In *Landscape*, there are two figures standing at the margin of an abyss of light. When he saw it, Tomlinson must have seen Adam and Eve and the Garden of Eden, a motif that flickers here and there into tenuous reification throughout his poetry. Nothing of the Garden or of anything else is specifically recognizable in the graphic, except that in one loop of light there is a tiny photograph of a coach and pair, which serves to give the whole picture gigantic proportions. But its very lack of specific images renders it more powerfully evocative than the controlled engravings of John Martin, for example, who illustrated *Paradise Lost* with meticulous detail; in Tomlinson's Eden, the mind is released into its own creative activity.

Eden, in various manifestations, haunts Tomlinson through all his volumes of verse. In one poem, "Eden,"[14] a "gift / Of forms" is one of its properties. Such a gift may be seen in "The Atlantic," the first poem of his first major work, *Seeing is Believing*: the opening describes light in a breaking wave; as so often, the poet seeks to contain moving light for a moment in a frozen scene. In "Departure," from *The Shaft*, published twenty years later, there is a similar image in which thought and moving water coalesce and momentarily freeze:

> it is here
> That I like best, where the waters disappear
> Under the bridge-arch, shelving through coolness,
> Thought, halted at an image of perfection
> Between gloom and gold, in momentary
> Stay.

Tomlinson, as will appear, knows that the static representation is false, but much of his oeuvre is an effort to trap the flux and to hold it in a moment of vision. In the section of *The Shaft* called "Perfections," in which "Departure" appears, the poems repeatedly present images abstracted from flux but containing "not all there is to be seen."[15] And if Eden is a gift of forms, one embodiment of it for Tomlinson is light caught by water and movement arrested.

Eden may be a species of purity, a nakedness. After "all ways of knowledge past," he says in "Glass Grain,"

> Eden comes round again, the motive dips
> Back to its shapely self, its naked nature
> Clothed by comparison alone—related.[16]

In "Frondes Agrestes: On Re-Reading Ruskin," from the same volume, Eden is

> the single grass-blade, or
> Gathered up into its own translucence
> Where there is no shade save color, the unsymbolic rose—

this idea in spite of Ruskin, who is cited in the same poem:

Light, being in its untempered state,
A rarity, we are (says the sage) meant
To enjoy "most probably" the effects of mist.

If Tomlinson's graphics leave much to chance and to the seminal opportunity of unstructured space, his poetry exhibits all the caution and control that art critics have found to be characteristic of contemporary British art, which is composed when, as at least American critics feel, it ought to be uncomposed.[17] Tomlinson, however, is very much aware of the field of discussion and the contemporary crises that have given rise in poetry to the avant-garde developments mentioned above that he intends to avoid. In particular, he registers his ambivalence as to whether the form in the poem is a feature of the real world or only of its representation. "His central manner of procedure," a reviewer notes, "is to observe . . . some natural object or process, till the brute continuity of the actual begins to seem like aesthetic necessity."[18] But form in the poem is often found in a reflection of the real, a reflection sometimes deliquescent. Indeed, images in water are ubiquitous in Tomlinson's verse. Reality is changed in the watery reflection, and it is ordered. "Swimming Chenango Lake" provides one example from *The Way of a World*:

a geometry of water . . .
Squares off the clouds' redundances
And sets them floating in a nether atmosphere
All angles. . . .
. . . .
It is a geometry and not
A fantasia of distorting forms.

The form in this and regularly throughout other poems is one discovered in an act of perception that is not mere innocent seeing. In "Swimming Chenango Lake," reality is ordered—only to a degree—but order is by no means the

final statement of the poem. The swimmer enters the lake
and achieves a vital union with it:

> he scissors the waterscape apart
> And sways it to tatters. Its coldness
> Holding him to itself, he grants the grasp,
> For to swim is also to take hold
> On water's meaning. . . .
> . . . .
> alone, he is unnamed
> By this baptism, where only Chenango bears a name
> In a lost language. . . .
> . . . .
> Human, he fronts it and, human, he draws back
> From the interior cold, the mercilessness
> That yet shows a kind of mercy sustaining him.

The swimmer is clutched by a cold reality, challenging the
previously noted patterns that formed an incomplete statement of his relationship to the scene: "not until they are
'scissored' apart and the unnaming baptism undergone,"
says Tomlinson, "is the experience complete and it does
not end with any comforting 'ordering' of reality: the lake
takes over from the poem."[19] He adds, moreover, "The
help we can gain from alien phenomena . . . is towards relation, towards grasp, towards awareness of all that which
we are not, yet of relationship with it. It is a help that
teaches us not to try merely to reduce objects to our own
image, but to respect their otherness and yet find our way
into contact with that otherness."[20]

The geometry Tomlinson frequently finds in scenes in
his poems may remind us of the geometry in the early Williams by means of which Williams tried to bring painterly
qualities into his poems to avoid the literary luxuries of
imagism inherent in a scene: in "To a Solitary Disciple," he
recommends that the angle of the moon, not its color,

should be observed. So Tomlinson, imagining Courbet might have painted a chrysanthemum, says,

> . . . he would have missed the space
> triangled between stalk and curtain
> along a window-frame base.[21]

Repeatedly, there is geometry: "The Tree" opens with a child, who

> knows nothing of the pattern
> his bent back lifts
> above his own reflection:
> it climbs the street-lamp's stem
> and cross-bar, branching
> to take in all the lines
> from gutter, gable, slates
> and chimney-crowns to the high
> pillar of a mill chimney.[22]

Form, however, need not be geometrical. "Foxes' Moon," included in *The Way In*, provides an example of the formalizing of a remote sensation about the night:

> These
> Are the fox hours, cleansed
> Of all the meanings we can use
> And so refuse them.

The concept of the human irrelevance of the hours of the night can be given a local habitation by integrating it with the life and times of the natural history of the fox: the night hours can be spoken of in terms of foxiness. Geometrical stabilizers are nevertheless present in the poem: "moonlight on the frigid lattices / Of pylons" and "shapes of dusk / Take on an edge." We may note also another formal quality and a regular characteristic of the later verse especially, a lovely reticulation of rhyme that spreads through the poem—rhyme, in Tomlinson's own words, "hiding itself among the syllables, in the bells and knots of language": [23]

> . . . foxes bring
> Flint hearts and sharpened senses to
> This desolation of grisaille in which the dew
> Grows clearer, colder. Foxes go
> In their ravenous quiet to where
> The last farm meets the first
> Row from the approaching town.

But the main process in "Foxes' Moon" is a formalizing in which objects are correlative not of emotion but of a sensation or an idea that calls for articulation. "In Connecticut" shows a similar strategy by the repetition of the word *white*: villages, churches, snow, sky, birch twigs, and rows of pillars all are white. And these organize the idea of candor and conviction with which a woman offers praise for a minister,

> delivered
> with the same shadowless conviction
> as her invitation, when
> lowering, leaning
> out of the window she was cleaning
> she had said: "Our doors
> are always open." [24]

Form is also conceived of as an ending. The last poem of *Written on Water* posits the satisfying form of the drama in which narratives and lives have endings, against the formless real lives of actors and audience: in "Curtain Call," "the dead" are called back from their dressing rooms after the end of the play, are reluctantly resurrected and forced to rejoin their "unplotted lives."

Finding the skull of a seabird on the beach, Tomlinson writes as follows: "The cleanliness, the natural geometry of the skull suggest the idea of surrounding it in a geometry of your own—carefully ruled lines that set off the skull, that extend it, that bed it in a universe of contrasting lines of force . . . skull and lines build up and outwards into a containing universe." [25] This represents a part of this poet's strategy: to supply the context of a design upon the world, to create a *containing* universe, by the "mind's imperious geometry." [26] It is, of course, to some extent an instantaneous and involuntary act: it is not the eye alone that sees the world but the mind, employing memory and creating structure from the anarchy of sensation. "The senses," Tomlinson says in one of his prose passages, "reminded by other seeings, bring to bear on the act of vision their pattern of images; they give point and place to an otherwise naked and homeless impression. It is the mind sees." [27] Indeed, "the mind is a hunter of forms." [28] In "A Garland for Thomas Eakins," a poem in *American Scenes*, the poet asks rhetorically,

> What does the man
> who sees
> trust to
> if not the eye? He trusts
> to knowledge
> to right appearances.

The accent is Marianne Moore's; later in the same poem, in the style of Wallace Stevens, the poet remarks,

> A fat woman
> by Reubens
> is not a fat
> woman but a fiction.

She does not absolutely represent the real, but she is the product of an ordering of the chaos of sensory experience.

In other poems that bring up the structuring power of the mind, Tomlinson frequently comes close to Wallace

Stevens. Turning his flashlight upon a stand of nettles, he recognizes the presence of an ordering power:

> What large thing was it stood
>   In such small occurrence, that it could
> Transfigure the night, as we
>   Drew back.[29]

And, again, as the poem closes with reference to the night:

>   The dead had distanced,
> Patterned its lineaments, and to them
>   The living night was cenotaph and ceaseless requiem.

The echoes are audible, from "The Idea of Order at Key West," "Peter Quince at the Clavier," or other poems in which Stevens endlessly questions reality and the transfiguring power of the mind. Tomlinson has a lover's quarrel with Stevens, asking, in the preface to the second edition of *The Necklace*, "was there ever a poetry which stood so explicitly by a physical universe and against transcendence, but which gives so little account of that universe, its spaces, patterns, textures"?[30] As concerned as Stevens to identify what the world is really like, Tomlinson comes to the problem not via Stevens but via the long debate on the nature of the visual impression—the question of the innocence of the eye, to use the metaphor of Ruskin, with whom he disagrees.

For Tomlinson, as a painter, the landscape or the static scene is the natural object for the poem. He cherishes a marriage between scene and action, especially in images that identify eye and hand in action—in the poem "Maillol," for instance, about the man who turned to "an art / where hand and eye / must marry,"[31] a man who became a sculptor. Tomlinson introduces action into his own art but does so, it seems, with little relish. He doesn't seem altogether at ease in reporting the awkward, jagged edges of detailed action. In "Mackinnon's Boat,"

> Macaskill throws
> To Mackinnon a cigarette down the length
> Of half the craft. Cupping,
> They light up.[32]

He is more successful when action is frozen into a tableau: the momentarily frozen wave in "The Atlantic"; the "Pompeian pause" that "arrests / Merton beside his window" in "The End";[33] or "Action unsinewed into statuary," in "Charlotte Corday."[34] In "Assassin," from *The Way of a World*, he imagines frozen lightning; in the opening of the title poem of that volume, he says he had forgotten but now, safe in the pluperfect tense, remembers,

> The image of a gull the autumn gust
> Had pulled upwards and past.

He does not conform to the precept Charles Olson underlined in his copy of Fenollosa, that "thing and action cannot be separated,"[35] but despite the necessary predilections of the painter, Tomlinson respects flux. Like Roy Fisher in this respect, he knows that reality cannot be caught in what is fixed: "if there must be / an art of portraiture," he says, for example,

> let it show us ourselves as we
> break from the image of what we are:
>
> the animation of speech, and then
> the eyes eluding
> that which, once spoken,
> seems too specific, too concluding.[36]

On the matter of form and order, Tomlinson's position is not simple. He apparently believes there is an order in things and he can speak, as we have seen, of "spaces, patterns, textures," and can go on to cite Hopkins's "'world of canon and fugue.'"[37] He also refers to the rhythm of writing as a "feeling out of the design," as "an inventing of the material, where material and design neither pre-exist 'just to be written down' nor exist in separation."[38] Whether parallels for his work should be sought in analytical cubism or synthetic, Cézanne or Juan Gris, is uncertain. He desires order to be found and held against flux but at the same time he is aware of the fortuitousness of the order: in a poem titled "The Chances of Rhyme," he says that these chances

> are like the chances of meeting—
> In the finding fortuitous, but once found, binding.[39]

Tomlinson is not unmindful in his poems of an intractability and an overwhelming disorder of the world beyond art, although in the poem just cited we are asked,

> why should we speak
> Of art, of life, as if the one were all form
> And the other all Sturm-und-Drang?

He fosters the kind of ambivalence that is similarly in *Paterson*; for Williams,

> without invention
> nothing lies under the witch-hazel
> bush,

but for him also,

> The rose is green and will bloom,
> overtopping you, green, livid
> green when you shall no more speak, or
> taste, or even be.

Tomlinson doesn't want to constrain the world into a rigid form or to annihilate reality into a heroic couplet, as Pope. In a number of poems, he finds language and the human faculties themselves incapable of meeting the fine shades of reality; though reality may "Ask words of us":[40]

> we
> believe our eyes (our lies)
> that there is nothing there
> but what we see.[41]

He recognizes the autonomy of the objective world even if he is too human to give it everything. In one poem, using Pope as an example, Tomlinson makes the point that Pope's sheer intelligibility bars the human approach, while an Aztec sacrifice, because it is a mystery and without boundary, "touches us more nearly."[42] The disinclination to regiment the objective world finds a parallel in his antipathy to the *merely* willed shaping that he warns against in the political poems "Prometheus" and "Assassin," both included in *The Way of a World*.

In the discussion about the painting of the skull, Tomlinson speaks of the "little universe my lines netted together around it," manifestly aware of the limitations involved in the geometrical strategy. He is questioning how he can relate that little system to the darkness inside the skull. Skulls engage him, bringing as they do the mystery of the intractable: "Skulls are a keen instance of this duality of the visible: it borders what the eye cannot make out, it transcends itself with the suggestion of all that is there beside what lies within the eyes' possession: it cannot be possessed."[43]

Because of that unpossessed reality, art is unable to achieve faithful organization of the real, a theme that finds its way in one various hint or another into many poems. There is the early poem "Sea-Change," a Stevensish exercise in which metaphors for the sea successively replace one another: "The sea is uneasy marble"; "The sea is green silk."[44] The poems ends,

Charles Tomlinson

Illustration is white wine
Floating in a saucer of ground glass
On a pedestal of cut glass:
A static instance, therefore untrue.

The static, which to be literal is all that poetry or painting can provide, is dismissed. There is a beautiful statement of the failure of art forms in "The Fox Gallery":[45] the upper story of the poet's house was so called because, window to window, one could follow the expected route of a fox, "parallel with the restraining line / of wall and pane." The geometry proved to be wrong, however: when the fox duly appeared, it came at an angle different from that expected—*toward* the house. So they watched it

> sheer off deterred
> by habitation, and saw
> how utterly the two worlds were
> disparate.

The two worlds, superficially animal and human, are more generally the real and the artificial; nature, we see, is not to be organized by our geometrical conceptions of it. Another poem, "The Chestnut Avenue," shows nature defying the conceptual limitations of the human arrangement:

> At the wind's invasion
> The greenness teeters till the indented parallels
> Lunge to a restive halt, defying still
> The patient geometry that planted them.[46]

We have lent them order, but "Mindless / They lead the mind its ways, deny / The imposition of its frontiers."

The fox in "The Fox Gallery" is described as "that perfect / ideogram for agility / and liquefaction"; so in a poet who leaves nothing to *mere* chance, we may identify this creature with the flowing process of life that Tomlinson is bent upon recognizing in a poetry that yearns, all the same, for the static scene. He pays homage to process. In the prose piece "A Process," he writes of the pictograph as "an outline, which nature, as the poet said [Henry Reed, one supposes], does not have."[47] Rain, in the same piece, is a process; and its "perfect accompaniment would be that speech of islanders, in which . . . the sentence is never certainly brought to an end, its aim less to record with completeness the impression an event makes, than to mark its successive aspects as they catch the eye, the ear of the speaker." We are reminded perhaps of the preliminary sketches of Leonardo or of the poems of Charles Olson, in which the early stages, the rough drafts of outlines or phrases that have been improved upon, remain along with the improvements. But if we compare Tomlinson with the American open-form poets whose actual *form* is process, then his homage to process seems controlled.

There is one feature he does share with them, however, which is perhaps more significant than the mere curiosity it appears to be: the affection for stone in the imagery. It is a paradox that poets who have jettisoned fixed forms and adopted fluid ones manifest this predilection for images of the most hard and permanent element. Or perhaps it is rather a compensation—of the same order as the recourse to *Emaux et Camées* as a model on the part of Eliot and Pound, recoiling from the excesses of free verse and "Amygism." In poets who present form as process, Williams, Robert Duncan in the *Passages* poems, Denise Levertov, and Olson himself, stone and its engravings are hard and permanent. In Tomlinson, the image of stone is only less ubiquitous than that of water. It is firm and fixed: the stone piers of "Over Brooklyn Bridge," for example, or the hardness of the face in "Portrait in Stone," both in *A Peopled Landscape*. Even in the same volume, however, stone, like scene and geometry, must allow for process:

"The Picture of J. T. in a Prospect of Stone" wishes for the child the constancy of stone:

> —But stone
>   is hard.
>   —Say, rather
>   it resists
>   the slow corrosives
>   and the flight
> of time
>   and yet it takes
>   the play, the fluency
> from light.

Water, however, is Tomlinson's favorite image, appearing especially frequently in *Written on Water*. It offers by reflection a picture of the world and sometimes of oneself. But as often as the poems present still, reflecting water, they present also running water. In "Logic," for example, water flows, and the ripple of a blade of grass on the surface destroys the image of the sky. The surface, moreover, is confused by rocks it flows over,

> humped by the surfaces
> It races over, though a depth can still
> And a blade's touch render it illegible

(the last word part of an image cluster in Tomlinson who, as in the title *Written on Water*, for one example, often links water with reading or calligraphy). We may expect the running water to be the figure for life itself, anarchic, haphazard, influenced, getting there in the end. But it proves instead to be a metaphor for logic—"for it flows / Meeting resistance arguing as it goes"[48]—the wayward stream standing for the epitome of rational order. Still and running water come together again in the title poem of *Written on Water*, which is part 6 of a sequence called "Movements." The "life lines of erratic water" are "hard to read"; there is also the "still pool"

> That we were led, night by night,
> To return to, as though to clarify ourselves
> Against its depth, its silence.

This is the penultimate poem in the volume, and it ends with a superb fusion of flux and constancy, the moving water and the images of stone that summarize these elements and their relationship for the volume:

> "Written on water," one might say
> Of each day's flux and lapse,
> But to speak of water is to entertain the image
> Of its seamless momentum once again,
> To hear in its wash and grip on stone
> A music of constancy behind
> The wide promiscuity of acquaintanceship,
> Links of water chiming on one another,
> Water-ways permeating the rock of time.

3

Roy Fisher

Roy Fisher teaches in the American program at the University of Keele, but for his own writing he finds nothing more influential in American poetry than its freedom. His work is significantly and largely concerned in both subject matter and manner with the avoidance of constraint. There are, for example, the constraints of city existence and of "the net / of achievable desires";[1] there are the constraints of rhyme, of contrived stillness and beauty, and especially of the conscious mind, all to be escaped. Of particular interest is the deliberate avoidance of such formal constraints as plot, or meaning, or relation to reality. Repeatedly, Fisher speaks of his work as free from the "entailment" to reality;[2] he is not interested in the kind of poetry that offers the comfort of a structured surrogate world. Indeed, meaning and its concomitant comfort are less important to Fisher than is "Making some kind of potentially new dislocative effect in the minds of . . . readers."[3] The strategies of this

---

Roy Fisher (b. 1930) has led a primarily academic life: a teacher since 1953 and until recently a member of the Department of American Studies, University of Keele, Staffordshire. He has not remained within the walls of the academy entirely, however. Among his outside interests is jazz, and Fisher has played piano in a variety of jazz groups since 1946. He was a painter and graphic artist when young, and his poetry maintains a tie to these interests. Some of his poems are extremely visual; they force the reader to *see* what is described.

poet work out variously in different volumes, but his comment on *The Cut Pages* (1971) gives the general idea: it was written, he says, "on sheets taken out of a notebook between whose covers I no longer wanted to work. The aim in the improvisation was to give the words as much relief as possible from serving in planned situations."[4]

Fisher was a graphic artist and painter as a child. And though his poetic work is linear and except for an early experiment not intended to be spatial, like Lee Harwood's poetry, he is still oriented toward visual art rather than books. Many of his poems bear a close relation to painting, and in these we can see that color and outline are often dissociated. The color may come first, before the shape: a doorway may become "visible as a coloured shape"[5] or there may be "a deep shining yellow / that plunges down with white enfolding it."[6] Sometimes color comes only in abstract forms, as "squares of colour" gleaming "across the suburbs,"[7] like the canvases of cubists.

In Fisher's early work, as well as in poems like paintings in which color has escaped its outlines, we find the equivalents of collages or assemblages: in *City*, called by Fisher an assemblage, the poet reminds us of the surrealism of Magritte, Dali, or Hans Richter and describes people "made of straws, rags, cartons, the stuffing of burst cushions, kitchen refuse. Outside the Grand Hotel, a long-boned carrot-haired girl with glasses, loping along, and with strips of bright colour, rich, silky green and blue, in her soft clothes. For a person made of such scraps she was beautiful." The standards for beauty are apparently moderate. In another passage, a tree is created out of "a great flock mattress; two carved chairs; cement; chicken-wire; tarpaulin; a smashed barrel; lead piping; leather of all kinds; and many small things." To some extent, Fisher seems to see his world as a painting, a collage, or an assemblage but even such minimal coherence as these possess may be too much for him.

City is a combination of poetry and prose, an assemblage, and thereby distinguished from *The Ship's Orchestra* and *The Cut Pages*, which were composed. It was "carved from half a dozen notebooks, poems written in various towns or about various towns or no town at all."[8] Fisher first made a symmetrical assemblage, but this was disorganized by Michael Shayer and thus published by the Migrant Press in 1961. Fisher subsequently reorganized the first version into a tidier one.[9] Parts of *City* are surrealistic, but often it is the precise and strange logic of a Kafkaesque dream that we seem to be following: "I sense the simple nakedness of these tiers of sleeping men and women beneath whose windows I pass. I imagine it in its own setting, a mean bathroom in a house no longer new, a bathroom with plank panelling, painted a peculiar shade of green by an amateur, and badly preserved. It is full of steam, so much as to obscure the yellow light and hide the high, patched ceiling. In this dream, standing quiet, the private image of the householder or his wife, damp and clean."

The poetic and prose passages of *City* are discrete; one could say it is a work with about thirty "things" in it. They contain images from the large industrial cities of northern England: vignettes, sometimes distorted, and views from curious angles such as through the spokes of the wheels of railway cars. Sometimes the scenes are illusory, and imagination is as real as reality. At night, the poet sees what he interprets as a couple embracing. It proves to be an engine driver, "probably drunk"; but not committed to a single perspective, the poet "could not banish the thought" that what he had first seen was the engine driver's own fantasy: "Such a romantic thing, so tender, for him to contain." Throughout *City*, there are repeated images of iron, concrete, factory walls, cisterns, girders, and streets. Nature is defeated mostly: birds sing against mechanical hammers; sickly grass and lean weeds spring from blue chemical soil. The city is still a casualty of bombing during the Second World War, and it is also the victim of its own decay. Images of destruction and desolation abound.

Sometimes the scenes express directly or obliquely the pathos of human life and its limitations in the narrow urban circumscription. Donald Davie says the poem is concerned "with a social reality, to the exclusion of the human,"[10] though this concern may be subordinate in the poet's intention to the expansion of feelings about the ideas of his forbears embodied in the planning or lack of planning in the city.[11] According to Davie, the sexual ecstasy of others horrifies the persona of *City*, and in the following lines, says Davie, the poet excludes tragedy: "Once I wanted to prove the world was sick. Now I want to prove it healthy. The detection of sickness means that death has established itself as an element of the timetable; it has come within the range of the measurable." In the few instances in which humans appear in the largely empty city, their noble potential is lacking; they are nobodies with "impacted lives" and unimportant qualities. The girl made of rags and miscellaneous scrap is judged beautiful; both here and in later works, however, humans are sometimes presented like those injured and humiliated humanoids that contemporary artists create out of kapok, papier maché, and miscellaneous junk. His relatives killed in the bombing were

> . . . marginal people I had met only rarely
> And the end of the whole household meant that no grief
>   was seen;
> Never have people seemed so absent from their own
>   deaths.

In lines quoted above, the poet sees humans in "tiers"; later they are deformed, diseased, or ashamed. They are shrunken. "Their significance escapes rapidly like a scent, before the footsteps vanish among the car engines." Another passage (in which the referent of *it* is uncertain) reads, "It could be broken like asphalt, and the men and women rolled out like sleeping maggots."

City has been compared with William Carlos Williams's *Paterson*, not surprisingly, since both are concerned with cities, in their titles at least, and both are on rivers. But *Paterson* is bland and frank; it lacks imaginative intensity and a sense of distress. Its prose passages are heterogeneous, whereas those in *City* are in a single style. *Paterson* lacks the occasional quality of dream, the obliquity, and the surrealism of *City*. In some respects, *City* is closer to *The Waste Land*: Eliot's vividly neurotic images, for example, of

> bats with baby faces in the violet light
> Whistled, and beat their wings
> And crawled head downward down a blackened wall

is recalled by the following, in the rhythm of a lyric in "East Coker."

> Subway trains, or winds of indigo,
> Bang oil-drums in the yard for war:
> Already, half-built towers
> Over the bombed city
> Show mouths that soon will speak no more,
> Stoppered with the perfections of tomorrow.

Fisher is elsewhere indebted to Williams, but none of the poets I address in this book is less indebted to Americans than Fisher, who is acclaimed in some British academic circles as their best living poet.

What might be compared with *Paterson*, however, is an identity between city and poet, explicit in *Paterson*, uncertain but hinted at in *City*. Dr. Williams might have said, as the poet of *City* says,

> . . . whenever I see that some of these people
> around me are bodily in love, I feel it is my

own energy, my own hope, tension and sense of
time in hand, that have gathered and vanished
down that dark drain.

But Fisher sometimes seems alienated:

> I come quite often now upon a sort of ecstasy, a
> rag of light blowing among the things I know, making
> me feel I am not the one for whom it was intended,
> that I have inadvertently been looking through another's
> eyes and have seen what I cannot receive.

He feels "a belief that he should not be here"; although
wishing to relate to his city, he is wary of endowing it with
a structure, a meaning, or a reality that is false.

In the prose passages describing it, the city is dominated
by linear images, handrails, railway lines, grooves, fences,
and especially streets radiating outwards, their layout
sometimes approximately revealed by gas lights or by the
moving taillights of cars. For the poet who as a boy lived
in an industrial city, "whose woodland walk was a gut-
terstone," who until he was thirteen never slept a night
outside blackened Birmingham, how might the streets
ever fail to symbolize the confined life? At any rate, Fisher
seems obsessed with the linear images, determining forces
that must be escaped. They are analogous to the outlines
from which the colors in other images have escaped.

The centers from which the linear images radiate are
empty, invisible, or decayed. In the first section, Fisher
mentions "the city's invisible heart," and the invisibility is
to be remarked. Later we read that the "great station" that
had been built at the end of the railway is now a goods
depot with doors barred and windows shuttered, men and
women too frightened to pull them down. One section of
the poem, titled "Starting to make a tree," describes the
preparations for the creation of the radial parts but for
the trunk there is left a clearing.[12] The void at the center of

these images is a symbolic rejection of unity and it is related to the repudiation of erotic ecstasy and tragedy, already referred to, both of which are totalizing, reducing multiplicity into a single order, providing the larger inclusive meanings that Fisher is busy to avoid. A section of *The Cut Pages* contains a curiously parallel utterance: "Centre. They brought a centre and set it up here, but it wouldn't take. It was rejected, and went off sideways." Michael Shayer, in his introduction to the first edition of *City*,[13] notes with approval the avoidance of unity which he had helped to ensure in this work. This avoidance of unity or the dominance, later, of a mere succession of sensations stands in opposition, of course, to the reader's instinct to discover order. And the poet's intention is baffled to the degree that one can say that the *point* of *City* is apparently made by the related images that paradoxically deny structure.

The occurrence of metaphor within the prose passages of *City* is so extremely rare that the literalness must be assumed to be a calculated effect. As it is an assemblage, the sections of the poem do not of course proceed in any narrative or logical order; and just as there is almost complete absence of metaphor in the texture, so in the structure there are no analogical relationships between the larger parts. One detail of a descriptive section in prose is found again in another section, not necessarily the following one, where it relates to additional details, these generally of an order different from those attending its earlier appearance, so that logic and an overall meaning are precluded.

Reality inheres in discrete items out of context: "Think of what all the people you see taste like and you'd go mad," the narrator observes in *The Ship's Orchestra*. If "you" go after the taste, it "is something that's always retreating; even if it overwhelms, there's an enormous stretch of meaninglessness in it, like the smell of the anaesthetist's rubber mask in the first moments—it ought to mean, it ought to mean; but how can anything mean *that*?"[14] And thus, although the narrator wants to believe "in a single world," as he puts it, at the same time he is committed to freedom from it: "I see the iron fences and the shallow ditches of the countryside the mild wind has travelled over. I cannot enter that countryside; nor can I escape it. I cannot join together the mild wind and the shallow ditches."[15]

In the poems titled *Ten Interiors with Various Figures*,[16] reviewers have seen the record of a relationship, a marriage perhaps. It is a failure, if not a drastic or irremediable one; the people are stuck with each other. The series looks a bit like a narrative, like *Modern Love* perhaps, from which the plot has been withdrawn, leaving only images. But, in fact, the poet did not begin with a narrative and then leach out the plot; he built up the sequence by repeatedly reworking basic images, taking as precedent the *Maids of Honor* series, in which Picasso made about twenty paintings out of the same set of images (derived from Velásquez). In some of the poems the narrator is a man, in others a woman; in a few, either. The repeated images around which the series circles are a sad inventory of the dull things that measure out our lives, to which, as if to burdens, the figures in the poems are painfully attached: light bulbs, packages, bottles, walls, jugs, hair, wallpaper, ill-fitting clothes, and tasteless brown furniture, brown food, and brown clothes. What is received from the poems even stronger than the sense of a failed relationship is the oppressiveness of these details, the items around which our days ineluctably revolve: not to be liberated from them is a species of imprisonment, yet they are at the same time, ambivalently, the very texture and sine qua non of life itself. The final poem in the series, "The Billiard Table," reveals the disparity between the two persons, for whom the physical phenomena on a billiard table provide quite different visions. Morning reveals that the table has been slept on: first, the mass of sheets suggests "a surgery without blood" (a vision shaped surely at some level of memory by Yves Tanguy or Marc Chagall); then, "you" glance at it until "the tangle looks like abandoned grave-clothes"; next, "I" see it is

> . . . the actual corpse, the patient dead under the
> anaesthetic,
> A third party playing gooseberry, a pure stooge, the ghost
> of a
>   paper bag;
> Something that stopped in the night.

At the end of the poem, however, the two come together in their mutual need of the commonplace and petty—the milk jug:

> Have you ever felt
> We've just been issued with each other
> Like regulation lockers
> And left to get on with it?
> . . . .
> Bring the milk jug, and let's christen it.

The five or six members of the ship's orchestra in the prose sequence so titled are confined in the ship, not permitted to perform. There are vestiges of narrative, but the characters have only the most sketchy backgrounds supplied and the elements of plot are too shadowy to elicit our questions. The narrative is not to be taken too seriously, Fisher says, because "it's not going to come together." The unrelated fragments of narrative in Kafka's journals are a model. Another precedent is *Kora in Hell*, in which William Carlos Williams brings together fragments of prose according to tenuous links of association. Of *The Ship's Orchestra*, Fisher says, "the book is written as an elaboration of almost hallucinatory sensory effects—tactile, olfactory, visual of course, auditory. . . . And it's an exploration of familiar body sensations. . . . And any intellectual play that takes place is meant to be seen as a possibly futile, bemusing, almost certainly erroneous play over the commands of a rule of sensation."[17] The sections of the work are without analogical relationship to each other; each was written, Fisher explains, "in an attempt to refer only to what I had already written in that work, and without any drive forward at all."[18] The narrator appears as himself, but there is also an actor playing him. Moreover, there is a sickly surrealist figure appearing at intervals, who seems, from one light hint, to be another form of himself. The separate brief passages of prose that constitute the book present, as we proceed, increasingly surrealistic visions, strangely compelling, which, in spite of Fisher's comments, shift our concern away from the actual objective elements to the subjective state of the narrator that they presumably notify. We are told in one place that the whole ship, in fact, "does not float; its parts are arrested in their various risings and fallings to and from infinite heights and depths by my need for them to be so."[19]

Sentences in the sequence tend to be short, sometimes laconic (slightly reminiscent of Auden's style in *Letter to a Wound*), and there is a punctiliousness in the accuracy of descriptions. In some respects, especially in its practice of taking up a motif, relinquishing it, and then taking it up again modified or from another angle, *The Ship's Orchestra* recalls Robbe-Grillet. Like Fisher's earlier work, it accommodates obsessions in its imagery: rings, white surfaces, and walls feature largely. At the center of the book, three or four passages are devoted to pipes and to a compulsive desire to destroy them (in part, perhaps, because they *are* at the center and constitute a system):

> Visceral pipes of white porcelain, huge things, in banks and coils, too wide to straddle. How to get lost in the morning.

They reach up in stubby loops and descend far beneath, the systems crossing, curving round, running in parallel. Some plunge vertically . . . some come creeping. . . . Potential fracture of the pipes. Virtually impossible. Only single-handed with a light sledgehammer, squatting on the topmost U-bend and clouting at the pipe until it cracks and shows the ochre stuff it's made of. Then bashing at the necks down to the levels, smashing across the fat conduits that curve down, caving in long sections of horizontal pipe from above, then standing in the channels and striking out at the sides.[20]

The section continues in this vein for another two hundred words.

In this work, feelings inhere in the shapes and colors that appear like the fantasies that come to one in a high fever. In one place for example, the narrator describes his body infused with light: "My body explored slowly by squares of differently coloured light. Odd sensation. The little slanted rectangles alter the sizes of the parts of my body they touch from moment to moment and leave a black creek of me in among themselves, that waves and shakes itself about in pursuit of them. The flapping black unseen part of me: a unity."[21]

Throughout *The Ship's Orchestra* there are images of destruction—of the performers' instruments, for example, and, as we have seen, of the pipes. The topic haunts the narrator: "All this disposal business, these basins, enamel buckets, plunging tubes, embalming sluices, constant jets, sterile bins, sealed incinerators, consideration of where the banjo-player might have gone that night, of the abolition of words taped to our memories, of the storage of one night under another night, the earlier ones gradually fading as the multi-track builds up beyond the bounds of desire; all this question of the attenuation of substance to concepts."[22] This "horde of destruction," to borrow from Picasso, is related to what appears in many passages: the false enclosure of perceptions in some arrangement, definition, or other circumscription, followed by their release. An image of a half-naked woman seated in a cane armchair on a plank bridge with handrails is followed by this: "Merret, Dougal [members of the orchestra], it is you and I who have put her there; struggling in our leather breeches through the mud of the site, carrying her at shoulder height in the cane chair."[23] Or there is the following, which comes closer than other passages to an explicit statement of strategy:

> The ship is a unity. Enclosed within its skin of white paint it floats upon, and chugs across, the unified ocean . . . to me it is a flat canister bearing another canister and a similarly cylindrical funnel, the basic canister shape being eccentrically elongated. . . . At any rate the ship is a unity and does one thing; it proceeds on its cruise. Not only does it have a structural and purposive unity; it has a music which proceeds with it, sounds within it and makes signals of the good life. In among the musicians is the tough glass bubble of the music. Reasoning, now. The musicians don't play. No bubble. The ship is not a unity. It is not white. It is grey, indigo, brown. Thin girderworks of green, and orange even, and coils of pale yellow piping. It is not a series of canisters; it is a random assembly of buildings. . . . The ocean is not a unity but a great series of shops turned over on to their backs so that their windows point at the sky.[24]

The musicians apparently must be prevented from playing and unifying what must remain separate.

Another significant image of destruction should be noted: among the many curious illogical details presented with the terrible seriousness of the dream appears now and again the sickly surrealist figure, a "white suit with a big orange on it for a head"—again, like the models of wounded humans in contemporary art. It is a figure of a helpless, wounded god, an authority figure become victim. Upon its second appearance, the difficulty of crucifying it is brought up: "The orange falls off. . . . The shirt collar feebly tries to mouth the last words; you replace the orange, it falls again. You can't put a nail through the orange to hold it to the cross; that's another story."[25] When it next appears, the head is bruised, the result not of blows but, like a Kafkaesque nightmare, of violent fondling. Then it is bandaged, carrying a stick; and, finally, the figure crouches in the washroom while a nurse removes the bandages. The narrator wonders whether it has been forgiven.

The volume *Matrix* appeared in 1971, containing the title sequence and others. "Five Morning Poems from a Picture by Manet" is earlier than "Matrix" and, though resistant to rational approach, less hermetic. There is more given in image and idea for the reader to hold on to; there are repetitions that give at least a rudimentary sense of structure; and there is a recognizable development between beginning and end. Fisher worked on this more than on other pieces; he wrote it in 1959 but held it back out of fear that it was overcooked. The sequence is based on a painting by Manet, "Boy with Cherries," but moves away from the one canvas into others and into imaginative constructions involving the four nonvisual senses. Its development is remarkable in the change between the first and last poems: the first offers a vision of the painting as an object of stillness and beauty, extracted from the live world by what Fisher calls the "generous eye," the creative mind of the artist; the last, like the opening poem of the "Matrix" series, presents the painting in terms of movement.

In the first poem, Manet's painting is imaginatively augmented to include trees and a shadowy stream:

> A drift of morning scents
> downward through pines
> dazzled, to hang on water finally;
> the road's deserted curve; beyond
> blue town-smoke standing.

The schoolboy is motionless, "cast in a pose of beauty." In the last poem, on the other hand, he is

Walking beside the wall towards the stream
where flickering water-lights
lick amber tongues quickly across stone,
with a yellow bag of cherries, an old jacket,
a red cap crumpled on thick hair.

In this same poem, the "sun walks down," and we see "smoke bursting," hear "silence dropping." Between the first and the last poems, the painting serves as departure for imaginative activity that brings a variety of constraints—marble, polish, art, stillness, beauty, understanding, and death. "The lately dead" of the second poem walk "with marble steps to iron trumpets"; "each footfall muffles breath, each iron grace-note / stoppers the heart with heartless beauty." In the third poem, the boy of the painting suffers beauty inflicted on him by the poet's creative faculty, his "generous eye," and rhyme or half rhyme dominates the images.

Trumpets of iron shake the sky;
in chains of ceremony they spill
out of the music of a generous eye.

Over his quiet they wear away
all to a frigid emphasis
on lines that form his child's flesh into beauty.

Slowly comes the polished step,
cut marble agony to blight
the charm of cherries and the scarlet cap;

to drag the forms of beauty till they gleam
dully.

The rhyme imposed here with the assertion of beauty comes again irregularly in the first three stanzas of the fourth poem, which presents conflict between life and mind—"Looking for life, I lost my mind"—and conveys the resentment of the dead. There is no reference in this poem to the Manet painting; instead, it presents the dead who have been "tricked and bamboozled by the world itself": [26]

Muttering, they told me how their lives
from burial
spiked back at the world like knives
striking the past for legacies of wrong—
the fiction of understanding worst of all.

The concluding stanza is in unrhymed verse, and the images now suggest the withdrawal of the creative function of the eye:

I saw a vase of familiar flowers
behind it, a tray
of thin pale brass with patterned borders;
the troubling taste of an alien mouth not figured
even in fantasy.

The fifth poem returns to the Manet painting and its additions. And now that the active mind of the poet has been quieted, the picture, as we have seen, is now full of life and movement; recognizing this effect, the poet apparently no longer wishes to observe a scene with his mind bent on beauty, for that approach is deadening. When the mind withdraws its "generous music," on the other hand, the scene takes on life.

"Matrix," like the earlier sequence, makes use of painting, as Fisher made clear on the dust jacket of *Matrix*.

The sequence of ten poems called "Matrix," from which the book takes its name, is probably the most developed piece of work in verse I have done, a comparatively rich mix of allusions and sensory imagery. Some while ago, without warning, I had one of those curious near-hallucinatory experiences in which one is able to stand outside one's mind and watch its oddly assorted memories quickly re-programming themselves to make new forms. On this occasion there was a rain of images which seemed to be joining one another according to some logic of their own. They were nearly all to do with works of art; and I could see impressions from Böcklin, Claude Monet, Thomas Mann and lurid tourist souvenirs from Japan, among many others, forming up into relationships which I should never have presumed to try to impose on them consciously. The complex collective image they made was still present after some months had passed, and the poems of the sequence are a sort of tour of its interior.

Fisher speaks of himself as having merely done the proverbial secretarial job in the making of "Matrix": he just wrote it down, having to leave it written as issued. But it is a poem he can return to for ideas, a matrix, in fact. "It is poetry about pleasure," he has said elsewhere; indeed, "There are actual pleasurable affirmations . . . which I did want to associate with body rhythms, falling, thrustings, risings and all that. I wanted to put that in, and they are sketched in in the structure there." [27]

In the ten poems in question, as in earlier works, there are colors free of outlines and shapes without meaning. We recognize immediately reflections from *The Island of the Dead* by Böcklin and the water lilies of Monet. There are, in addition, images of islands, between which are clefts of silver sea, gardens with ravines, and rocks with fissures. One could suggest a general assignment to these: the gardens and islands reflecting stasis; the fissures, freedom and movement. The clefts and ravines are bridged. There are paths, spirals, snail shells and a cochlea, gauzelike fabrics, and surfaces of rock and water—but all a bit insubstantial. Among these images is that of a drop of fluid, derived from an incident in Mann's *Dr. Faustus*, into which "the dwindling emerald waters" are drawn, "as if, past all extension, / to the devouring drop." In another poem in the volume, the poet turns a little abruptly from landscape to a worn black pebble in his pocket, which is traced with veins like the streets in *City* and which seems to have the similar power of devouring movement and freedom:

> Once
> I watched it ingest
> a violin concerto
> of Bartók entire.[28]

Fisher's dust-jacket comment describes a kind of creation in which the mind was able to watch itself. It is not unusual to find Fisher thus divided, seeing himself in one form or another. "Matrix" is not the result of pure automatism—it is not hallucination itself but an unstructured "tour" of the "interior" of the "complex collective image." He called this his most developed work, and it appears that what he achieved is an escape from the control of the conscious mind: the poems, if not pure surrealism, are not ones the poet would have presumed to write consciously. There are earlier places where he touches briefly on the state of freedom from conscious mental activity. In a prose passage in *City*, for example, he expresses ambivalence about its power over things: "In this city the governing authority is limited and mean: so limited that it can do no more than preserve a superficial order . . . fuel, water and power. . . . This could never be a capital city for all its size. There is no mind in it, no regard. . . . Most of it has never been seen." Not to be seen is a kind of achievement. In addition to this hint about mind, the need for freedom from performance is also touched on earlier: "The Poplars" (a poem in *City*) where the poet speaks of his "net / Of achievable desires," concludes,

> All I have done, or can do
> Is prisoned in its act:

> I think I am afraid of becoming
> A cemetery of performance.

In the matter of freedom, however, there is an even closer concern in an early poem, "Toyland," originally part of *City* but later excluded,[29] which concludes with a patronizing description of the Sunday activities of citizens:

> For the people I've seen, this seems the operation of life:
> I need the paint of stillness and sunshine to see it that
>   way.

Elsewhere, this technique seems to be one that he wants to avoid. The last poem of "Matrix" suggests that visual clarity, product of the stillness and sunshine previously required, is no longer a need.

> There's a time, finally,
> when it doesn't matter
> that the rings of the eye
> slacken, and won't mark
> so many differences.

At the end come these lines,

> whole surface on the move
>
> filtering currents
>
> tangled with trailers
> of sky, and maybe lilies,

as if, again, the poet aligned stasis with mind and to them opposed life and movement.

What the critic is to make of the poems in this sequence, containing images of which the relationship, not consciously arrived at, is by no means clear, is no mere academic question: for the critic not only is the literary bureaucrat with his categories and forms to fill out (and whose questions the poet does not always answer), but he is also a part of each reader who instinctively seeks relationships and order. A *TLS* reviewer found that *The Ship's Orchestra* gained from the richness of its fantasies and lost with their pointlessness.[30] As we have seen in Fisher's comment on that work, the poet does not propose to offer the kind of point sought by the reviewer, who might well have made the same comment on *Matrix*. The effect of this poetry, as with a good deal of other contemporary work, is of dissatisfaction, which coincides with the poet's avowed interest in a "dislocative effect" in the reader. The dislocation, achieved throughout "Matrix" by the general loss of coherence and relation, is also brought about as each poem typically moves away from its initial statement, which is often a reflection of a detail in a painting. Thus, from a water gate presented in the first poem of the sequence, the poem moves into a metaphor within a metaphor and then into considerations that are irrelevant:

> Alone, it could be a house,
> chin on the water,
> hat-roofed. . . .
> or was it the last thing built
> of all the provisions
> in the pattern—
> the one lacking purchase
> and pushed on to the waves?

Or perspective may suddenly shift from a survey of a painting into consciousness of words, as the internal rhyme in the following from number 3 sharply withdraws us from a study of the image:

> . . . always the same dead
> seem to be walking.
>
> Spectres of respect.

Occasionally what is given may be most peremptorily taken away: in number 5,

trenches of silver water pierce
the island-cluster
or do no such thing.

The dislocative effect is brought about in the texture of
the poem by small acts of mutual cancellation between
words. As noted above, for example, Fisher alludes to
paintings, which are by nature fixities; as if anxious to
breathe life into them, however, he has sometimes presented items not in painterly terms but as if they were
alive and capable of movement or as if they were the ends
of processes other than acts of painting; in number 1,

. . . it gives footing
first on to rock

where channels cut shadow . . .
. . . was it the last thing built
of all the provisions
in the pattern—
the one lacking purchase
and pushed on to the waves?

Number 2 offers this example:

Levelled, the chasms filled
pinnacles snagged off,
skimmed with a surfacing
that cakes into a path.

Sometimes an incongruous modifier distorts or destroys
the usual meaning of the substantive, disrupting the for-
mation of a crystallized impression: there are "padded
scents" of flowers; "Eight or nine yards / of offered crossing"; walls "built with old money"; "Slatted sounds." In
many passages, including this one from number 5, no single image or single meaning materializes:

Spiralling from the shore
in blocked paths and on dropped

or jutting levels,
the stations of the thing
face over one another.

And, in number 8,

Blood-red and blue glass
stain the air thinly
on a deep turn:

maybe it is approach.

Coherence leading to meaning or to a visual image is not
always lacking. But often the first and obvious literal meanings and qualities of words do not convey experience,
lines such as "glass veins of music in the flesh" and "Religious garden / dropping between two gables," for example; and the context does not indicate which meanings are
to be appealed to or how to elucidate the figures. A reader
may not recognize allusions to paintings and previous literature, or the symptoms of Ménière's syndrome in the
ninth poem, or how all these fit together. The poem is not
easily accessible, as the poet is aware; he recognizes also
that accessibility is not by any means the whole point. Although a reviewer may complain that there is a failure in
communication, "Suppose—," the opening poem of the
volume, not part of the "Matrix" sequence, should show
us that Fisher is intent to preserve us (one is tempted to
add, at *all* costs) from habitualization, the universal depres-
sant that in Viktor Shklovsky's words "devours objects,
furniture, one's wife, and the fear of war,"[31] and should
show us that the poet will demand our cooperation in using the old to procure the new. In "Suppose—," somebody
finds a poem:

The old flat arrangement,
Dry track of half a voice—
And lets it drift on his own thoughts,

> Like a simile. . . .
> This used idea, abandoned
> And pinched up into caricature,
> Monitors and shakes the new.

Fisher thereby proves himself to be backing away from any system by which a poem, a picture, or an image may be frozen into formal beauty. He works consistently at the edge, where the stillness of beauty gives way to life, or vice versa. His wish to be thus metaphorically at the edge is reflected in a favorite image that recurs throughout both poetry and prose—standing on the edge of a cliff or bluff with the land falling away into distance.

This predilection for standing on the border between art and life contributes to the arrangements in the prose pieces in *The Cut Pages*. The pieces in one set, "Metamorphoses," are, in the author's words, "exercises in changing, in full view, one thing into another whose nature was quite unforeseen at the outset, the change to be worked by playing over the starting idea until it began to loosen and dissolve, and yield place to another which looked as if it had a right to be there. The point of interest for me here was not so much the ideas as the slowed-down exploration of the kind of field in which ideas exist, and the ways they have of succeeding one another."[32] The result bears comparison again with the associative method of Williams's *Kora-in-Hell*. "Metamorphoses" consists of five pieces, each with three to six sections. The second one illustrates how one thing "yields place to another." It begins by describing a cat staring up. The second section describes the distance in the cat's eyes: "Running into the distance there's a dull aluminum strip of road, tall skies, flat horizons, with scattered elms and poplars picked out in colour by the sun." The last section of the piece removes the scene to what is seen from passing cars—a white drum-shaped water tower, a cinder patch, and a path. The third piece in "Metamorphoses" shows a man in an ill-fitting suit, his departure from the "rigidly composed scene," and finally the sudden freezing into stillness of the figures in a movie, as the film ceases to move in the gate and commences to burn. Fisher's characteristic treatment of image is here embodied: the last section begins, "No system describes the world. The figures moving in the background stop and wait in mid-step, the sound-track cuts out. . . . Among the whites and greys of the picture a golden shade is born."

"Stopped Frames and Set-Pieces," another series of prose pieces in *The Cut Pages*, includes one or two minutely described frozen actions—"fragments the eye cannot read," a note explains, "while the machine can": a boxer dog caught at the peak of a leap, a man dancing with a balloon over his head. Paintings, by Francis Bacon, once again provide a close parallel. Fisher's extracted fragments of action, not responsible to any context, are related to a description in the same series of a small, broken Indian statue, given in intricate detail at considerable length. The poet is characteristically content to remain with the fragment: "There's no temptation to guess at the positions of the vanished head and limbs." Sometimes among these vignettes he is content also to remain with a physical appearance unqualified by moral considerations; in one piece of prose, "long runs of blood flowed" from the dead, following a street massacre, "right down into the gutters. Its brightness was astonishing, the gaiety of the colour."

In this sequence and in other prose pieces collected in *The Cut Pages*, Fisher presents carefully described scenes or actions. Occasionally, they are of flying; conversely, they often show figures confined—in a weird sort of water bath, in an underground bar that becomes a cavern in the body, while drowning, or when buried in earth. The images of flight and burial come together in a tale told in "The Flight Orator," in which there is a thirty-foot bird, king of the little birds, a traditional situation in allegory. The large bird wings his way sorrowfully over the land, presiding over human dreams. "He flies low, it's all he can do to keep going: saving his strength for the hills, and the tall forests and the long stretches of water," until finally he lands and sinks into the earth. Here there is a "strong temptation" to guess at the meaning of the allegory—that it points to the poet, his sad condition, and the cessation of his traditional role. But we should note also that the bird is, again, a figure of a failed god, like the victim in *The Ship's Orchestra*.

"The Cut Pages," the title piece of the volume, was "taken forward," the poet says, "with no programme beyond the principle that it should not know where its next meal was coming from. It was unable to anticipate, but it could have on the spot whatever it could manage to ask for. This method produced very rapid changes of direction."[33] The point of the writing was the act itself as a means of breaking out of a block that had inhibited creation for about four years. There are fourteen pieces, each longer than those in "Metamorphoses" and containing many more units, which, individually, are much shorter than those in "Metamorphoses." The following is an example, the opening of the work and selected by Fisher to read in a recorded interview:

Coil	If you can see the coil hidden in this pattern, you're colour-blind
	Pale patterns, faded card, coral card, faded card, screen card, window fade
Whorl	If you can see this word and say it without hesitation you're deaf
	Then we can get on with frame
Frameless	Meat-rose, dog-defending, trail-ruffling

Dodge

The Redcliffe Hotel? Forget it

A critic sees *The Cut Pages* as moving from "fragments of actuality to a sense of cosmic mystery" and claims it has a religious impulse.[34] Fisher has emphasized that there is no referent outside the writing, no paradigm, and decreed that readers, curiously preserved from any "fiction of understanding," must give up the usual expectations. Fisher says his readers should let the words come and should see what sticks in their minds. The work obviously speaks, almost exclusively, to the needs of the poet himself, indifferent here to public or publication.

Personal need has again been the occasion for some of the poems in Fisher's latest volume, *The Thing About Joe Sullivan: Poems 1971–77*. In the twenty sections of "Diversions," for instance, the words and images seem to be born out of a need associated with such phrases as "the old paths trouble knows," "my own dark," and others. Another poem, "If I didn't," contains these lines:

> there's always
> the looking down
> between the moving frames
>
> into those other movements
> made long ago.

One such "movement" is the poet, half his lifetime back, on Goodrington Sands, "troubled in mind," his trouble objectified in the look of the beach as he is walking:

> acres of sandy wrack
> sodden and unstable
> from one end to the other

The poems of *The Thing About Joe Sullivan*, however, though they may suggest fulfillment of a need, do not encourage its analysis. Most of them illustrate again the principles noted above that govern Fisher's latest work prior to this volume. There is the familiar resistance to a controlling meaning, which is precluded, for instance, in "107 Poems" by the scrambling of images. The poem consists of 107 lines that contain the scattered elements of what was or what might become a narrative. But it is not a narrative. It brings to mind, on the other hand, the notion of William Carlos Williams (adopted from Marcel Duchamp) that a stained glass window is more interesting when shattered and lying on the pavement than when it is in its frame.

Some poems proceed by association, as before, one thing yielding place to another that "looked as if it had a right to be there." They proceed as if the words came first and then caught whatever meaning they might—a process upon which Williams, again, in passing at least, set his approval. "Timelessness of Desire" reads in part,

> There is only, without a tune,
> timelessness of desire.
>
> don't open up the way
> this town shines in through glass
> and the days darken.

Sometimes associations lead to a logical incongruity: "From the Town Guide" begins,

> Out in the air, the statue
> gets cold. It needs a coat.
>
> The coat must have a face on top
> to squint for dandruff on the shoulder

—an image that takes us back to those curiously patched-together anthropomorphs of *City* and *The Ship's Company*.

"Barnardine's Reply" avoids the story of the dissolute old prisoner whose life is spared in the general fifth-act amnesty of *Measure for Measure*. Yet in its images it catches the atmosphere and important sensations at the end of that play. There is, for one thing, the musky redolence of the whole unsavory, sexy atmosphere: "The veined breast with its risen nipple," and Venus flexing her back to be mounted

> wordlessly, like a hunting dog—
> just for her scent
> and for the look in her eye.

There is the marvel of the light into which the old convict is released: "the prisms divide and subdivide, / the caverns crystallize out into day." There is the mystery of that light and his new world: he came out

> into a dawn world
> of images without words
> where armed men, shadows in pewter,
> ride out of the air and vanish,
> and never once stop to say what they mean.

Perhaps something of the poet's own feeling about the play, the world, and, hence, the need behind the poem is expressed without much obliquity in a final image of Justice, "gagged with its blindfold / and wild about the eyes."

Barnardine's experience, let out into the light that for us shines on everyday things but for him on a world of fresh images unjaded by meaning, is the experience of this poet. The poem contains much that is characteristic of Fisher's work and shows also something of the height to which his style can rise.

4

Matthew Mead

Like Roy Fisher and a number of other contemporaries, Matthew Mead writes poetic sequences. These constitute a large proportion of his work, and they may be compared with those that are best known in this century, *Hugh Selwyn Mauberley* and *Life Studies*, each of which contains autonomous poems that together present a theme. Mead's sequences are closer to the former inasmuch as they lack confessional material but contain fictions as *Mauberley* does; they differ from both models in the obliquity of the contribution of individual poems. In "Identities,"[1] the poems reflect some of the conflicting claims and concerns or embody certain elements of a complex self that the poet is concerned to express, to know, and perhaps to integrate. Many of the poems are ironic—comments on political or social scenes and some ironic *Frauendienst*. There is a nonironic poem of parting, a love lyric, a poem in the mode of a Roman elegy, and one poem that could be called a collage. All these are linked, sometimes by miscellane-

---

Matthew Mead (b. 1924) is the former editor of *Satis* magazine (Edinburgh). With his wife, Ruth, he has translated Bobrowski, Bienek, Borchers, Sachs, and Sabais. He has called Sabais's *Generation* "the important poem by a contemporary." Mead's is a European consciousness, well aware of its place in the decline of the West. Mead now lives in West Germany.

ous imagery common to two or more of them, regularly by their contribution to the themes of love, ferocity, human cruelty, and violence on the one hand and identity on the other.

The first poem of the sequence introduces us to the names of places and men associated with cruelty:

After Paeschendale
After Katyn
After Auschwitz
After Kronstadt
We stand here

After Asquith
After Beria
After Noske.

In the second poem, the poet parts from his girl. The next presents the poet as a figure like Gletkin, the inhuman interrogator in *Darkness at Noon*. In 4, he is a salesman of a product, which proves to be himself. Poem 5 is a lyric with an intricate rhyme scheme in which the poet asks, "Am I not also a candidate for fame?"

I sing
To be in her song-
ster-plume
one feather
Plucked.

The sixth poem implies that the body, the body itself, is a man's identity, but it then declares,

The one promise worth making:
Immortality.

And finally, "Body: metaphor for death." Number 7, after the style of a Roman elegy, describes how the poet has been invited to dine at the table of a rich man where he is faced by the specter of the unfed "hordes of the East." He suggests sending the host to the "lands of morning. / He serves a very good dinner. / He may meet cannibals." Of all the poems in the sequence, the eighth speaks most directly to the themes of identity, suffering, and cruelty, the poet identifying himself with characters from *Tristan and Isolde*—Tristan, Morold, Melot, Kurvenal, and King Mark, who both inflict injury and death and are the victims of it. Being part and parcel of the cruelty and the suffering of the age, the poet asks:

> How then shall I drink
> and lie beside you in life
> and lie with you in death?
>
> Or are we singing some other opera?

Allusions such as these emphasize that the theme in the sequence, although there is a good deal of specific political reference, probes a fundamentally human subject. Other sequences in *Identities*, including "A Poem in Nine Parts," though they too assert their human relevance, have a more striking political coloration and remind us that Mead has, in his own words, found that "the failure of socialism has been important to [his] verse."[2]

The ninth poem in "Identities," in a completely different tone from that of 8, is an address to secret police organizations by an officer arguing the therapeutic value, after torture has been inflicted, of a "good burst / from a submachinegun." Poem 10 presents examples of religious and political conflict that have resulted in one kind or another of execution—the religious disputes that brought Hus to the stake; political disputes involving Pombal, St. Just and the King, Marx, Lenin, and Trotsky. In each of the three stanzas, Mead submits a pragmatic motive for the dispute, asking serially what there is besides loot, profit, and satisfaction. Number 11 begins, " 'You must meet Julie, oolala,' " and develops into an ironic comment on the flesh, related perhaps to these lines in 6,

> To resume from this dust the loved flesh
> as from scorched clay the monsoon rains
> wrench a brief tribute of green.

Poem 11 concludes by juxtaposing the allure of the flesh with its ephemerality.

> I must meet Julie. Oolala.
> So many other girls are dust.

Number 12 is a collage, presenting first an image of the double nature of man: the leopard-men, like lycanthropists, presumably, who, while at night they are killers, in the daylight are very ordinary men—"Blunt-fingered, with only a little hair." Later in the poem comes the line, "Identity is a problem for pretenders," not, that is, the men of daylight. But we are all pretenders—artists, poets, lycanthropists—and the poem warns us of the imminence of oblivion:

> Unless he can, wreath piled on wreath,
>   Sustain each honour;
> Unless he can, plain title and clear proof,
>   Speak truly, word and echo;
> Each name is grey with breath
>   —an alias forgotten.

The last poem, 13, presents the artist, who traces "Through sham and sweat / a still-life without reflection," as lacking the delicacy with which frost lays patterns on the windows. Here, apparently, death is the artist whose patterns are supreme over those of the human:

> Tongue-tip and finger-tip touch silence, zero.
> Filigree leaf and star must draw the light
>   To their design,
> Dead rhythms of darkness

Dance through halls of flame.
Night must sing in the dawn crystal
And when the pane is blind with light
All this must be set down.

This outline gives some idea of the wide variety of subject and form in the poems of the sequence and the contribution each makes to the skein of interwoven themes. Besides the themes, there are other tenuous links between the separate poems: the repetition of images or phrases, the image of the "whorled ear," for example, or the clause "we stand"; the line "Regretting a bright head or a brief beauty" in 12 referring respectively to St. Just, mentioned in 10, and to the shapely Julie in 11; the appeals throughout to silence, darkness, death, and the rejection of the human body—its dimensions in 6, its vulnerability in 9, its curves in 11, its identity even in 12, and finally its inability to create in 13.

Mead's sequence, although its individual poems are mostly conventionally formed, is a relatively open structure that accommodates items on various topics and of various pitch, tone, and mood, loosely assembling them around a theme. Outwardly, "Identities" brings together poems of social and political comment with those of love, poems celebrating the living flesh with those idealizing whatever is beyond it—the spirit, immortality, or death.

The grouping of these poems into a sequence is a bringing together, as much of an integration of the self as can be achieved. But in spite of pervading themes and images, the title suggests that the *poems* are identities—the separate selves of the poet, with their separate concerns and promptings, the flesh and the spirit, and, more significantly, the poet's personal identity and his European consciousness. The intention is, perhaps, the arrival at a personal identity via not only consciousness but conscience, the acceptance of his own share of guilt for Europe's pain.

The problem is particularly characteristic of the 1930s, expressed, for example, in Stephen Spender's *Vienna*, in which private and public are unsuccessfully brought together, in the works of John Lehmann, Rex Warner, Bernard Spencer, and others who dramatically confronted the pleasures of the good life with their consciousness of political evil and the suffering it entailed and who so frequently quoted Keats, from *The Fall of Hyperion*, declaring that no man could usurp the heights of art except "those to whom the miseries of this world / Are misery, and will not let them rest." For Mead, although his wit is never entirely subdued, it would seem to be a desperate effort: he has "a really live sense of what it is like to live in a society where the direction of life has fallen into the hands of malevolent or ignorant functionaries, where all human values seem to be threatened by inhuman organization."[3] How to live, how to be whole in such an environment, is his problem, as it was that of intellectuals in the thirties.

On the contemporary scene it is not only Mead's problem, though Mead, living on the continent, is perhaps more aware than his English colleagues of the burden of the tragedy borne in Europe. The problem of how to be whole is central also for the poet Heinz Winfried Sabais, a member of a political opposition party in East Germany who fled to the West in 1950. Mead has thrown some light on his own attitudes by remarking, "The important poem by a contemporary is, for me, Sabais's *Generation*."[4] He and his wife have translated "Generation" and other poems by Sabais that show a strong historic consciousness and the contemporary collision between "Cubic colossi of iron" and "a man without a chance."[5] In "Elmo's Fire," Sabais's speaker is conscious, on leaving his woman, of her scent on his neck, but he is conscious too of the hard world:

In my blood . . .
forced-labour brigades struggle

with shivering fir-trees. Ah, inescapable
exile, nailed by shots
behind the edge of the forests.

In "Looping Above the West," the speaker is in a plane asserting his identity, free of the world:

Slender rocket into the last
deserts of freedom. . . .
To be I, without splintering skulls
To be I, without smashing-in ribs—
Space!

But the freedom is only momentary:

. . . startled red signals glow
on the watchful instrument panel.

And he is again "Imprisoned by the horizon / Looping above the West." Of all Sabais's poems, "Generation" especially seems to be written out of a bitter historical consciousness, in which memories of the Second World War and outrages in contemporary Europe still control responses:

Say: Flowery mead and we
think of fox-hole and
entrenching tools. Say:
Man—with Schiller and
Pascal—and we associate
exactly: stomach-wound, execution,
political police and all the
cunnings of self preservation.

These lines might have come from Lehmann, Spencer, or Warner. Sabais, we are told, writes to inform rather than entertain. His terrible political consciousness seems, whether shared or derived, to be Mead's.

Often in *Identities*, in failing light, Mead may exclude the world and focus entirely on the loved woman, as he does in a poem to "Tatania" and elsewhere, but love in declining daylight is frequently juxtaposed with political realities: in "Three Simple Things," for example "the hand that cups the breast / would finger the 'world-pulse'"; later, sleeping after love, the woman cries out of her nightmare, "Die Russen kommen." "For the rehabilitation of N. I. Bukharin," part 3 of the sequence "In Eyes of the People," which gives title to the volume that includes it, the poet presents, with some searing contempt, an image of the blind compliance of the myrmidons who acceded to the death and, in turn, the rehabilitation of Bukharin. That said, Mead withdraws in the following poem into the shadows where love presides.

The strategy of the sequence is appropriate to Mead's conscientious unwillingness to seek his identity apart from the forces of social and political evil around him; in the sequence he can not only present the multifarious self with restraint and decency but also bring together incompatibles that would break the mood of a single poem. A lyric poem by Mead is not ruined by the introduction of incompatible elements, as the mention of driving belts, for example, destroys the pitch of Stephen Spender's "The Funeral." The fourth poem of Mead's "A Poem in Nine Parts" ("Aide-memoir for an archetype of the Dark Mechanic"), without prejudice to the lyrical passages in other poems in its sequence, opens

> carpark officeblock and drive
> timeclock yard and railway siding
> puddle duckboard rusty castings
> gantry on a greasy sky.[6]

Only one line in the poem mentions human things: "flesh of wife and fear for children." "Aide-memoir" is ironic; the Dark Mechanic, destructive of the human, needs none.

The individual poems in "A Poem in Nine Parts" are, nevertheless, more closely related than those in "Identities." The sequence is concerned with freedom and industrial enslavement. Freedom is in the gift of the "Lady," or "she," or the "Winter Queen," who by one title or another is called upon in various poems. Her absence is related to unfreedom, in particular to the plight of factory girls who appear in two of the poems going uphill to work in "clock-numbered captivity":

> Because she does nothing
> the girls go up the hill
> against the wind.

The girls and their plight point to the theme of industrial slavery in an ordered socialist state. The Lady is associated with the moon, in one poem by a pun: "The moon withers in state." She is associated with silver light and repeatedly with the cold, one of the hazards of freedom readily accepted by the poet, who prefers her to the regulation comfort of institutional heating.

The repeated images and the theme link the poems of this sequence more closely than those of "Identities." Personal guilt is another theme of "A Poem in Nine Parts," with the poet, who in "Identities" had described the torture of an old man, imagining,

> The fingers, closing on a throat,
> Seen suddenly as hairy, not our own;
> And then our own. And ours the rage
> Masking amazement at the broken face
> Swaying before us as we strike again.

He hears his "traitor self / Cheer a proposal to delete compassion." There is an ambivalent attitude to the flesh: although the poem speaks of the "sweet flesh" of the girls, human flesh more often seems distasteful with its "[a]nimal pungencies" and the girls "mummd" and "tampaxt." There is some witty word play:

When in this monolithic state
I find your dress above your knees
Chloris my rising shall equate
Your needs to your abilities.

But there is also a turning away from the fleshly human condition in general. Indeed, one aspect of freedom is freedom from the body in death, noted in the following passage with its pure echoes of *Ash Wednesday*:

Mistress of fortune
    preserve our fortune,
Ruler of darkness
    prepare a death
for the flesh which sings now
makes moan and shivers silver
as the moon renews her light.

It will have been noted in some of the passages quoted above that among the sections of "A Poem in Nine Parts," and for that matter elsewhere, throughout are passages of melodrama—a feature noticeable in some of the English poetry of the thirties and perhaps inherited therefrom. Like so much of the poetry from that era, this is the poetry of protest, and strong feeling is occasionally on the loose.

Hey yeeorgi, Georgi Karpov!
Does the committee still meet Wednesdays
To smash the occasional ikon?

Again there is strong feeling with uncertain attachment in the following fairly typical lines:

Trumpet again the triumph of Soviet steel
Bring back the springing flesh of ballerinas
That the spectre of communism be seen
    only in public rooms.

A later sequence, "The Administration of Things," from

a volume with the same title, is more homogeneous, in tone at least, and more closely knit. It is a somber piece for the most part, though there is always wit—for example, the play on the words of the prayer book:

> warm thigh wet crotch
> salt hips and scent of hair
>
> Remember now thy creator
> in the night of his little death.

The sequence repeats the terms *darkness* and *death*, with the latter often used metaphorically to suggest the existence imposed by a totalitarian bureaucracy. Abstractions prevail throughout the poem:

> They have found order
> and they enforce order.
> A frame to hold the living and the dead.

But the pervasive darkness of the poem is occasionally lit by an image out of memory presented in an inconsequential flash reminiscent of Ezra Pound:

> And what the dead men saw I see—
> Girls on the lawn beneath a female sun,
> Breasts, thighs, the prison of bright shade;

or

> A smell of living—
> dark limbs in the darkness
>
> My hand cupped the breast
> hard-nippled
> and I remembered the flesh.

Memory dies, however, toward the end of the sequence. A sequence published in 1977, a poem in five short parts called "The Midday Muse,"[7] is closely knit by repeated images—of sun and light, shadow, sand, fire, and knives—

that play against each other in different relationships as the last words of the lines of a sestina.

"Three Simple Things" is a poem in three long parts,[8] but each part contains in itself sections that are as distinct in form and subject as the separate poems in some of the other sequences. The epigraph reads:

> ". . . . under her fingers order grew out of chaos; she established sequence and precedence; the symbols before her became coherent, interrelated."

Relationships in the poem, however, are to be articulated by the reader, "her" influence being apparently somewhat in abeyance. It is a poem about love, but it leads from descriptive poetry to a species closer to act itself. The first part, "To put a muse to sleep," dwells on the poet's fame and then presents the conflict between love and work:

> if I came to bed now
> the throat of a girl in Pitesti
> would lack the song which shall praise you
> in a summer you will not see.

A lyrical passage follows, then the lines already quoted concerning the respective claims of the breast and the world pulse. Subsequently, the sex act is presented, in present tense, suggesting that the poem is becoming an act:

> I enter . . .
> I wait . . .
> I move . . .
> and thrust, and this
> is love
> and this
> and this
> and this
> is love.

The other, outside world is forgotten. She sleeps, but in her dream she cries out, "Die Russen kommen."

Part 2 of the poem, titled "To Redistort a Weltanschauung," presents ideas of romantic youth and its betrayal by age and necessity, the resignation of the human will before the inexorable nature of things ("would you riot against the hoar-frost / or behead high noon?"), and the death wish in seven varied but not separated sections. In dwelling on these, Mead includes some images of nuclear preparedness about the globe, characteristic of this poet whose vision is never undarkened by political considerations. In the last section of this part, echoes of Pound are heard again:

> . . . light excels without object
> folding no form in gold
> in lazy splendour
> nor swift in the slash of air
> quick limbs leap and turn
> as men like gods in sunlight
> race down to the clear water;
> and no face feels the light
> burning and firm upon it,
> no eye seeks the line of hills.

In part 3, "To Love," there is an even stronger effort than in part 1 to get beyond the normal descriptive usages of language, commencing with two epigraphs: the first from Robert Creeley, "Love, what do I think / to say. I cannot say it"; the second from Sidney Keyes, "Make love another language." The latter proposes what Mead has attempted here: the actual verse opens with a lyrical passage in stanza form, beginning, "To love with love for love's sake only love"; in the following twenty-three lines *love* recurs forty times. The effect of the insistent repetition is "semantic satiation,"[9] by which the word is deliberately drained of meaning because the thing itself—love—is beyond language. Later, as in so much contemporary poetry in which silence is employed as the only possible means of expression for what is beyond words, Mead defines his love in terms of antithetical relationships; we understand through opposition.

> Speech by silence
> dark by light
> she by absence
> thus to know her.

The whole poem may be considered open, largely because of the unconstraining context in which the most various constituents appear—images and statements about love; allusions to John Donne and "The Canonization"; images relating to identity; the conflict between poetic creation and sex; the howling political world looming over the edge of consciousness; and superb lyrical passages, including the following (which shows, incidentally, how well Mead employs the negative, as Ezra Pound, his master, did before him):

> Or light has no likeness
> born of the same fire,
> no eye seeks the line of hills
> nor follows unthinking grace
> nor tongue trembles to truth
> ". . . . like gods to clear water."
> Nor is pride. Not the heart sick.
> Nor a name covered with darkness

—all these dancing in a permissive choreography.

Mead's conception of identity that cannot be detached from the cruelty and the strictures of contemporary history confines him in "Identities" to a sequence of formal utterances. As a whole, however, the method of the sequence lends him some of the advantages of poems more obviously unstructured in that he is able to accommodate such variety as we have seen. Furthermore, the marked differences in forms and rhythms reveal the differences in the selves of the poet and their respective moods more sharply than would a free and open form. The method of "Identities" is one solution to the problem faced by some of the poets represented in this book and others like them: how to provide structure and at the same time avoid its domination.

5

Geoffrey Hill

The impetus for a poem by Geoffrey Hill is metaphoric. He *realizes*, he says, not in situations or themes but in terms of metaphors. The metaphor is the starting point; the poet must find its true context, the poem, by conscious intellection. His poetry is difficult, and for the awestruck and embarrassed reviewer, most certain of its merit and most uncertain of its meaning, the dictum of T. S. Eliot that poetry may communicate before it is understood has come conveniently to hand. In an age in which much poetry moves toward openness, this is closed. Although many contemporary poets call for the creative contribution

Geoffrey Hill (b. 1932) is another poet who has led the double life of academic and artist. After taking his B.A. from Keble College, Oxford, in 1953, Hill began a teaching career that was to continue at the University of Leeds until 1980. He taught at the University of Michigan, 1959–1960; spent a term at the University of Ibadan, Nigeria, 1967; and held a Churchill Fellowship at the University of Bristol, 1980. Hill is currently University Lecturer in English and Fellow of Emmanuel College, Cambridge. In 1971, he received two awards: the Whitbread, and from the Royal Society of Literature the W. H. Heinemann Bequest. Hill was elected a Fellow of the Royal Society in 1972 and an Honorary Fellow of Keble College, Oxford, in 1981. His books have been honored also: *For the Unfallen*, the 1961 Gregory Award; *King Log*, the Hawthornden Prize of 1969 and the Geoffrey Faber Memorial Prize of the next year; *Mercian Hymns*, the Alice Hunt Bartlett Award for 1971; *Tenebrae*, the Duff Cooper Memorial Prize of 1979.

of their readers, Hill controls his in that complementary
exercise; Hill would not speak as Harwood does of readers
establishing *individual* readings for themselves, creating,
in effect, a number of different poems. More than many of
his contemporaries, Hill knows how he wants to be read.
And while many contemporary poets deliberately avoid
depth, behind a single word in Hill, there may be an ocean.
The word is not the correlative of an act, as in some recent
poetry, nor replete with primal energy; it is packed with
meaning. It is no coincidence that of all its predecessors,
Hill's poetry recalls most acutely the somber music of Allen Tate, who was aware early of the new trends but whose
late work, even, is strictly of the older tradition.[1]

A poem of Hill's may exist in relationships between elements that are neither logically connected nor necessarily
to be received chronologically. He favors, for example, the
sequence (like Matthew Mead but not for precisely the
same reasons), in which, while the sequential nature of
the arrangement is not remarkable, the meaning of one
poem is colored by its reaction against others. He uses titles, subtitles, and sometimes even dedications and epigraphs to qualify various parts of a poem, and that poem
may be said to comment upon these elements. The last
poem of a sequence titled "Of Commerce and Society" (a
title that comes from Allen Tate's "More Sonnets at Christmas, 1942," quoted in the epigraph to Hill's series) is preceded by passages that create a kind of field: the poem's
title, a dedication, and an epigraph. If we are to perceive
all its irony, we must read the poem with all these elements in mind, along with the title of the whole sequence:

> VI *The Martyrdom of Saint Sebastian*
> Homage to Henry James
> *'But then face to face.'*

The poem then begins:

Naked, as if for swimming, the martyr
Catches his death in a little flutter
Of plain arrows. A grotesque situation,
But priceless, and harmless to the nation.

Consider such pains 'crystalline': then fine art
Persists where most crystals accumulate.
History can be scraped clean of its old price.[2]

The martyrdom of the saint, popularly thought to have been effected by archery and made the subject of Renaissance paintings, is travestied in the first two lines, "Naked, as if for swimming" and "Catches his death," the common idiom for getting a cold. By cleaning the picture, "History can be scraped clean of its old price," that is, of sin and the commerce in the general title; "priceless" is also related to commerce, though colloquially it suggests "funny"; "a little flutter," referring immediately to arrows, can also have the commercial meaning of an adventure either on the stock market or at the race track.[3] "Crystalline" and "fine art" one may associate with Henry James. The cleaning process relates ironically to spiritual transformation, seeing not as through a glass darkly but face to face, the expectation of St. Paul, who is quoted in the epigraph.

The poem is an extreme example of Hill's practice of spreading out points of reference between the parts of a poem and its context, a practice sufficiently characteristic to warrant notice of another instance. The body of the poem "Ovid in the Third Reich" from Hill's second volume, *King Log* (also collected in *Somewhere Is Such a Kingdom*), reacts against the two elements in the title and an epigraph from the *Amores* in which Ovid declares that any woman is innocent unless she confess her guilt. The poem opens,

I love my work and my children. God
Is distant, difficult. Things happen.

The reference to the Third Reich in the title and the spurious innocence recommended by Ovid in the epigraph serve to draw out of these apparently innocent, inert lines the terrible history of the concentration camps.

The elements within a poem itself, themselves often obscure, may be related by links similar to those that connect epigraphs and titles rather than by an explicitly logical progression. Hill's practice of issuing points of reference that react against each other is not incompatible with the idea of the poem as music, a medium that naturally transcends its necessary temporality. We designate literature as musical when there are remarkable melodic effects of vowels or consonants (as in Tennyson, "mouthing out his hollow oes and aes," or in "Brag, sweet tenor bull," in Basil Bunting's *Briggflatts*), or, more significantly, when the literary structure is based on specific musical models (as in Strindberg's *Ghost Sonata*, for example, and Eliot's *Four Quartets*). We also refer to literature as music when we don't quite know what else to say about it—an alternative to Eliot's dictum about understanding and communication.

In an essay, "Funeral Music," Hill says about the sequence of the same title that he was "attempting a florid grim music broken by grunts and shrieks."[4] There are, to be sure, melodic passages in the sequence, "Fire / Flares in the pit, ghosting upon stone," and resounding clashes of vowel and consonant,

> we are dying
> To satisfy fat Caritas, those
> Wiped jaws of stone.

Perhaps it is rather a choreography of motifs and images, related to a theme and free of logical advance, that Hill's comment invites us to notice. The sonnets dwell on the human condition, its solipsism, the fallen flesh to which the aspiring soul is ineluctably wed, the pain of earthly existence and its inconsequence in the soul's history—an awful Manichean vision. The main theme, the conception of this world as "restless / Habitation, no man's dwelling-place" and life as a lingering pain, is set in the first poem:

> Processionals in the exemplary cave,
> Benediction of shadows. Pomfret. London.
> The voice fragrant with mannered humility,
> With an equable contempt for this World,
> 'In honorem Trinitatis'. Crash. The head
> Struck down into a meaty conduit of blood.

Much that follows in the sequence is here anticipated. "The exemplary cave" is Plato's cave of shadows, and the conception described by that allegory fits the pervading theme of *contemptus mundi*. The moving figures that make the shadows on the stone wall in the fable are by extension the historical figures in the procession that moves through the sequence, "Creatures of such rampant state," as they are later portrayed. Pomfret was the scene of the putative murder of Richard II, which preceded the civil strife of the Wars of the Roses (the second sonnet begins, "For whom do we scrape our tribute of pain— / For none but the ritual king?," reminding us of *2 Henry IV* in which the Archbishop turns insurrection to religion "with the blood / Of fair King Richard, scraped from Pomfret stones"), the castle being adjacent to the site of the Battle of Towton, one of the major battles of those wars, which appears here in the sequence. London was the stage for the beheading of John Tiptoft, Earl of Worcester, to whom the sequence is dedicated, along with the Duke of Suffolk and the Earl Rivers, all of whom suffered beheading during the second half of the fifteenth century—three lords, powerful men, lovers of the arts, whose fortunes once high had revolved on the wheel. The voice and what it says belong, as the essay informs, to Tiptoft, who commanded "that he should be decapitated in three strokes 'in honor of the Trinity.'"[5] The fate of his head, unmitigated by his piety, contributes to the theme running throughout—the grievous lot of humankind on this earth, the "stark ground of this pain."

References to the Wars of the Roses swirl about the central Manichean theme and provide a smoky glamour. Other motifs reflect each other throughout in idea or image clusters: fire and stone are associated, torches and atonement, armies and flashing light, blindness and reconciliation, trumpets and purification, silence and innocence.

A second theme in "Funeral Music" is the duty of the poet in relation to the demands of the dead to be reported aright in the world. The poem's function is to cleanse the past, to liberate history from the stain occasioned by its association with putrescent flesh and sin. The motif has already been glimpsed in "The Martyrdom of Saint Sebastian"; we see it again when, for example, "The lily rears its gouged face / From the provided loam." The poem's act is one of love; as death frees the soul from its earthly bondage, so the word may free history from the tainted mire of human veins—hence the relationship between the instrument of death and the angel that brings the word, as the three lords "dispose themselves to receive each / Pentecostal blow from axe or seraph." The theme of poetry as an act of cleansing is announced in the second sonnet,

> For whom do we scrape our tribute of pain—
> For none but the ritual king? We meditate
> A rueful mystery; we are dying
> To satisfy fat Caritas

(the "tribute of pain" and "dying" must surely be taken to refer to the creative act, to the making of poetry), and reflected throughout the sequence: "trampled / Acres" are "blanched by sleet"; darkness falls over the human mire; a vision of life controlled by intellect shows "an unpeopled region / Of ever new-fallen snow." Beyond the sonnet sequence, also, Hill's work is pervaded by the craving for purity, for the antisepsis of the mind as opposed to the corruption of the body, and for the cleansing of the past so that it may reappear as in childhood's innocent kingdom, purified by time and returning into the present as a part of a harmony. The sixth sonnet of "Funeral Music," for example, looks back through a child's vision to idealized images of men.

> My little son, when you could command marvels
> Without mercy, outstare the wearisome
> Dragon of sleep, I rejoiced above all—
> A stranger well-received in your kingdom.
> On those pristine fields I saw humankind
> As it was named by the Father; fabulous
> Beasts rearing in stillness to be blessed.

Although the poet has this duty of love to perform, poetry is nevertheless an act performed in pain or even disgust. It is occasionally associated with claws, as in "Words clawed my mind as though they had smelt / Revelation's flesh." And ease is reprehensible; the first part of "Annunciations," again, from *Somewhere Is Such a Kingdom*, closes in contempt of the trencher fury of respectable poetasters:

> all who attend to fiddle or to harp
> For betterment, flavour their decent mouths
> With gobbets of the sweetest sacrifice.

The second part, on the other hand, closes with lines on the theme of painful creation, the burden of love:

> Choicest beasts
> Suffuse the gutters with their colourful blood.
> Our God scatters corruption. Priests, martyrs,
> Parade to this imperious theme: "O Love
> You know what pains succeed; be vigilant; strive
> To recognize the damned among your friends."

The act of going into the past and bringing history into an innocent childhood kingdom in the present, noted above, produced in 1971 a sequence of prose poems, *Mercian Hymns*, in which the duty to history hardly seems a painful one. The sequence opens:

> King of the perennial holly-groves, the riven sand-
> stone: overlord of the M5: architect of the his-
> toric rampart and ditch, the citadel at Tamworth . . .
>
> . . . contractor
>
> . . . .
> to the desirable new estates: saltmaster: money-
> changer . . .
>
> . . . .
> "I liked that," said Offa, "sing it again."

The poems are to be regarded, Hill says, as commentaries on the subjects supplied by the headings. The so-called headings are not set each above its own hymn but are gathered separately in both *Mercian Hymns* and *Somewhere Is Such a Kingdom*. Almost all the headings relate the individual poems to episodes or activities in the life of Offa, eighth-century king of Mercia, to his attributes, or to legacies of his reign. In a few poems, the content does not concern Offa directly: number 14, headed "Offa's Laws," presents the persona of a West Midland rural magistrate; number 25, "Opus Anglicanum," is a lament for one of the old nailers of Bromsgrove, a town in the English Midlands. The headings are not rubrics but elements in juxtaposition to the parts of the poems proper, after the fashion noted in the earlier volumes. The parts of the poems, generally two, three, or four in number, set off as separate paragraphs, are themselves thus loosely related to each other in many of the poems. Individually, they may be clear and in this respect quite different from the elements in earlier poems; but the connections between them are often obscure, subtle, and tenuous.

Connections may be effected, for instance, by a motif derived from connotations or etymologies or from the fifth dictionary meaning of a word. Poem number 20 is headed "Offa's 'Defence of the English People'" and has only two parts. The first presents the "primeval heathland" with the bones of mice and birds, where "bees made provision, mantling the inner walls of their burh." The second is as follows:

> Coil entrenched England: brickwork and paintwork
> stalwart above hacked marl. The clashing prim-
> ary colours—'Ethandune', 'Catraeth', 'Maldon',
> 'Pengwern'. Steel against yew and privet. Fresh
> dynasties of smiths.

The small brick houses and bungalows with clashing colors are only too familiar on the English scene, but they are, each of them, the Englishman's home, his castle; without undue exercise of the fancy, they may be thought of as speaking to an England defended, "entrenched," and now presumably at peace. They are "stalwart," which comes from the Anglo-Saxon *statholwyrthe*, meaning having firm foundations. A note draws attention to the popular use in England of the name of ancient battles for suburban houses. The battles are presumably the foundations upon which England now rests, so that now the peaceful domestic art of clipping the hedge may supersede the art of war. But with the association of the battles, "hacked" and "clashing" take on a fighting sense; "smith," here primarily a common English surname, becomes associated with steel; and "steel," no longer merely the garden shears, suggests ordnance. Then the battle connotations reach back to the first part of the poem, where against a background of battle—the heathland strewn with bones—the bees, like the Englishmen, embellish the walls of the "burh," etymologically a fortress.

The eleventh poem, "Offa's Coins," has four parts and shows a similar reticulation formed by underlying meanings and associations of words. The poem has four parts; the first part and selections from the others are as follows:

> Coins handsome as Nero's; of good substance and
> weight. *Offa Rex* resonant in silver, and the
> names of his moneyers. They struck with account-
> able tact. They could alter the king's face.
>
> Exactness of design was to deter imitation; mutil-
> ation if that failed.
>
> Swathed bodies in the long ditch; one eye upstaring.
> It is safe to presume, here, the king's anger.
> . . . .
> Seasons touched and retouch-
> ed the soil.
>
> Crepitant oak forest where the boar
> furrowed black mould, his snout intimate with
> worms and leaves.

A selection of the connecting links includes those between "struck" and "anger," "struck" and "mould," altering the face and "mutilation," "tact" and "touched," "design" and "seasons," "soil" and "mould," and "ditch" and "furrowed." The association of coins, corpses, and the soil is discussed below.

"The Offa who figures in this sequence," says Hill's note to the whole book, "might perhaps most usefully be regarded as the presiding genius of the West Midlands, his dominion enduring from the middle of the eighth century until the middle of the twentieth (and possibly beyond). The indication of such a timespan will, I trust, explain and to some extent justify a number of anachronisms." Parts of individual poems apparently disparate may in fact be related through the identity of the poet in the three roles he plays throughout: himself, himself in childhood, and Offa the king. In number 29, "The Death of Offa," the penultimate poem of the sequence, the poet as child plays ludo (a game of dice and counters) with his grandmother and enters "into the last dream of Offa the King." In the preceding poems, the poet as child has slipped into identification with Offa while daydreaming, sometimes to return anticlimactically to the schoolyard where "the children boasted their scars of dried snot," at others to retain the royal elevation and impose it on his own world. In one poem, when struck on the head by an apple root, he momentarily becomes the horned Celtic god Cernunnos; otherwise, it is Offa who supplies the ego-ideal. Offa has the attributes a boy might covet, fame, wealth, power, and a GT car, an accessory that bestows status on English youth, hankered after, perhaps, by the young Geoffrey Hill whose father was the police constable of a West country village. In number 10, the boy as king at the royal desk, dispatching royal business, becomes the boy at his own desk doing homework. The poem is headed "Offa's Laws" and opens with a description of the desk. The second part mentions some of the official business transacted at the desk, using a few portentous latinisms:

> It was there that he drew upon grievances from the
>   people; attended to signatures and retributions

—activities that a child might imagine as the kingly function. The third part of the poem leads specifically back to the point of view of the child:

> What should a man make of remorse, that it might
>   profit his soul? Tell me. Tell everything to
> Mother, darling, and God bless.

The final part contrasts the freedom of daydreaming to work:

> He swayed in sunlight, in mild dreams. He tested the
>   little pears. He smeared catmint on his palm for

his cat Smut to lick. He wept, attempting to master *ancilla* and *servus*.

The poem has moved from official acts of Offa to the private acts of a boy doing homework, from the use of latinisms to the frustration over the mastery of Latin, from the
service of the king—the grievances of his people—to the
idea of *ancilla* and *servus*, a motif brought up in the epigraph to the poem, which appears in the André Deutsch
edition but not in *Somewhere Is Such a Kingdom* and which
considers the subject of government and the difference between a man's acting for himself and acting for others.

The poet descends regularly to childhood, to its warmth
and security, to the easy availability of forgiveness and
innocence. In the twenty-second poem, Hill recalls that
warmth and security—amid the contrasting images of war:

> At home the curtains were drawn. The wireless boomed
> its commands. I loved the battle-anthems and the
> gregarious news.

(During World War II, the BBC's nine o'clock news on Sunday evenings was preceded by the national anthems of all
the Allies.)

> Then, in the earthy shelter, warmed by a blue-glassed
> storm-lantern, I huddled with stories of dragon-
> tailed airships and warriors who took wing im-
> mortal as phantoms.

Having thus gathered the innocence of childhood, the
poet comes grandly back into the present as Offa, whose
dominion endures, as we have seen, into the middle of the
twentieth century.

A number of the hymns present artifacts: the desk,
"brown-oak inlaid with ebony"; the tapestry, "the silver
veining, the gold leaf"; the Frankish sword, "the crux a
craftsman's triumph"; the coins. Some of the hymns pre-

sent the act of creation, analogous to the poetic act. In Hill's earlier poems, the poetic act brings its creations from the past, as in "Funeral Music," or from the soil, as in "The lily rears its gouged face / From the provided loam," and burnishes them. In the hymns, however, creations from the earth and the past are joined; the coins in number 13 provide one example.

> Trim the lamp; polish the lens; draw, one by one, rare
> coins to the light. Ringed by its own lustre, the
> masterful head emerges.

The creative act is signaled also by the presence of men working in the earth; in number 12, they dig up a hoard of treasure. Men with dirty boots are present in the second part of 23, following the description of the tapestry in the first part, tapestry and working men relating to creation. Finally, in the last poem, summing up essential relationships, coins and traces of red mud are left behind as Offa vanishes:

> he vanished

> he left behind coins, for his lodging, and traces of
> red mud.

The hymns repeatedly return to images of earth—soil, compost, and ditch—and to the creatures of earth—worm, badger, and mole; there is always digging or burrowing among roots. Indeed, the child's kingdom is most often underground, regularly earthy, as in the "earthy shelter" in the quotation above (which portrays an air-raid shelter, presumably). In number 5 we read, "I wormed my way heavenward for ages amid barbaric ivy, scrollwork of fern." The thirteenth shows the child emerging from earth to become the king, a poetic act.

> Far from his underkingdom of crin-
> oid and crayfish, the rune-stone's province, *Rex*

Totius Anglorum Patriae, coiffured and ageless,
portrays the self-possession of his possession,
cushioned on a legend.

The image of Offa in these lines is the one on the coin.
In the Mercian hymns, coins are, first, among the famous
legacies of King Offa's reign, and they bear an imprint of
his head. Second, they are frequently the treasure hoarded
underground. Note, for example, the presence underground of the gold solidus (a Roman coin) in number 4,
the heading of which is "The Crowning of Offa," a poem
in which *invested* is rich in meanings.

I was invested in mother-earth, the crypt of roots
and endings. Child's play. I abode there, bided my
time: where the mole

shouldered the clogged wheel, his gold solidus.

The same motif of underground wealth appears in poem
number 6, "The Childhood of Offa," which echoes the
rhythms of Dylan Thomas's "Fern Hill" and suggests a
complex relationship between active and passive participation in the events of time and the things of the world:

The princes of Mercia were badger and raven. Thrall
to their freedom, I dug and hoarded.

Coins are related to another feature of the poetry. In earlier poems the pain of poetic creation is often associated
with the attempt to break out of confinement. In "God's
Little Mountain," from *Somewhere Is Such a Kingdom,* the
speaker says he "was shut / With wads of sound into a
sudden quiet." In "The Bidden Guest," from the same volume, the poet speaks of Pentecost:

I believe in the spurred flame
Those racing tongues, but cannot come
Out of my heart's unbroken room.

Often the poet's sense of being pent up is associated with riches: he is shut up guarding a hoard. Alternating with this sense is that of release, and these two create a rhythm that becomes familiar throughout the volumes, in which images of confinement and pressure repeatedly precede those of relief. Hill has spoken of the wonderful sense of consummation and release that lasts for four or five seconds when a poem is completed. But the completed poem is still important to him: he is not finished with it when it is finished; he broods over it still. Hill is unlike Basil Bunting in this regard, who can say of his own completed work that once it's made, he's done with it. Another early poem found in the *Somewhere Is Such a Kingdom*, "Solomon's Mines," contains the characteristic imagery in its characteristic pattern: there is an underground hoard of riches and there is the sense of restraint and confinement. The poem opens with the line, "Anything to have done!" and closes as follows:

> Anything to get up and go
> (Let the hewn gates clash to)
> Without looking round
> Out of that strong land.

The image cluster of restraint and money may conceivably be related to the parts of the repeated word *Pentecost, pent* and *cost*, in spite of its proper etymology—a suggestion that will not be thought overreaching by those who have noted Hill's constant and profound use of puns and the depths of meaning that can be plumbed in individual words.

The pattern of hoarding, of confinement and restraint, followed by release, is even more clear with "In Memory of Jane Fraser," also in *Somewhere Is Such a Kingdom*. In the first three of the four stanzas, the images of immobility and confinement prevail: cold weather, "She kept the siege," the room, "Her body froze." In the last stanza come movement and release:

> In March the ice unloosed the brook
> And water ruffled the sun's hair.
> Dead cones upon the alder shook.

In a volume in which meaning is hidden away like the miser's coin, this poem is relatively clear and the clarity may account for its disfavor in the eyes of the poet.[6]

The coincidence of the pattern of restraint and release with images of treasure, coins, and corpses, and, in turn, the Freudian association of these last with feces, has a significance worth noting. The coincidence appears occasionally in Hill's poems or is hinted at in the overtones of brief passages; in "Requiem for the Plantagenet Kings," for example, "the sea / Across daubed rock evacuates its dead."[7] The act of poetry itself is at times a part of this cluster of images. In "History as Poetry," Pentecost appears, then the corpse, and then dung:

> Poetry as salutation; taste
> Of Pentecost's ashen feast. Blue wounds.
> The tongue's atrocities. Poetry
> Unearths from among the speechless dead
>
> Lazarus mystified, common man
> Of death. The lily rears its gouged face
> From the provided loam. Fortunate
> Auguries; whirrings; tarred golden dung.[8]

The last phrase recalls Freud's reference to Babylonian doctrine that regarded gold as the dung of hell.

Mercian Hymns, with the predominance of the coin images, also reveals these associations, which may serve to link the parts of individual hymns. Coins have already been seen in association with corpses in number 11. Number 12 presents a digging that is both an excavation for treasure and a utilitarian plumbing job. In the first part, "Their spades grafted through the variably-resistant soil. They clove to the hoard." In the second, "The men were paid to caulk water-pipes." These men have a latrine, and in the third part of the poem, describing the condition of the garden and bringing together the two earlier parts, the poet declares, "I have accrued a golden and stinking blaze."

Release from restraint may take the form of a journey in the Mercian hymns. In the seventh poem, "The Kingdom of Offa," Ceolred has let the poet's valued silver model aeroplane fall through the floorboards "into the rat-droppings and coins," after which the speaker lured him

> down to the old quarries, and flayed
> him. Then, leaving Ceolred, he journeyed for hours,
> calm and alone, in his private derelict sandlorry
> named *Albion*.

In poem 17, "Offa's Journey to Rome," after remembering a quarrel with his father and the curious "Disfigurement of a village-king," the poet finds relief in his sports car: "His maroon GT chanted then overtook. He lavished on the high valleys its *haleine*"—a word, according to Hill's note, taken from *La Chanson de Roland*. Visiting Boethius's dungeon (number 18) he purges himself of violence by violent imaginings:

> He shut his eyes, gave rise to a tower
> out of the earth. He willed the instruments of
> violence to break upon meditation. Iron buckles
> gagged; flesh leaked rennet over them; the men
> stooped, disentangled the body.

> He wiped his lips and hands. He strolled back to the
> car, with discreet souvenirs for consolation and
> philosophy.

It is interesting that each occasion on which the poet finds release in a car (or lorry) contains an act of sadism or disfigurement.

This is one of the more curious of the image clusters that link some of the Mercian hymns and other poems in Hill's canon. The hymns are also dependent on the relation of the king's activities to those of the child and of modern England to historic Mercia. The childhood of the poet is superimposed on the childhood of his country, and both are radiant as the poem celebrates England: history is lit by shining, finely cut coins, by tapestry with gold leaf, by a sword reflecting winter sun; the poet's childhood is romantic with badger and raven, the Rolls Royce, the GT, and life in the air raid shelter. All through the work, density and fine reticulations of meanings lend a definite structure to poems—unfashionable techniques, bearing Hill's unfashionably grievous message.

Tenebrae, Hill's latest work, retains some of the features of *Mercian Hymns*. There is, for example, the dwelling on buried things—treasure and corpses in the grotesque rendering of Christian salvation in "A Pre-Raphaelite Notebook"—"Gold seraph to gold worm in the pierced slime." There are occasional images and anecdotes reminiscent of the style established with the hymns. In "Vocations" "The twittering pipistrelle, so strange and close, / plucks its curt flight through the moist eventide." Mostly, however, the images do not recover a visual experience; rather, the words are felt as words with histories, objects themselves, not agencies. The volume is a reversion to the style preceding *Mercian Hymns* (a reversion predicted by Harold Bloom [9]); there are the tight forms, the rich elegance, the inaccessibility.

The condition for the poetry of *Tenebrae*, as for the earlier, is the maintenance of a balancing act between declaration and reticence, between the necessity of arriving at formal verse and the imperative of obscurity. Some of the sequences here are religious meditations, and the balancing is performed in the use of metaphor to bring what is ineffable not quite into expression but toward it. The management is particularly that of St. John of the Cross, whose influence along with that of other Spanish poets is evident throughout this volume. Hill's reticence reflects a comment of St. John's on one of his own poems: "It would be ignorance to think that sayings of love understood mystically such as those of the present stanzas, can be fairly explained by words of any kind."[10]

In the title of the opening poem of *Tenebrae*, "The Pentecost Castle," "Pentecost" carries the sense of harvest, and the wheat being harvested is a figure for Christ at His crucifixion. But the overtones provided by punning are in harmony with some of the hidden meanings of the sequence, in which satisfaction of desire paradoxically resides in satisfaction withheld. The epigraph, taken from one of Yeats's letters, initiates the paradox: "It is terrible to desire and not possess, and terrible to possess and not desire." Hill's strategy here is comparable with that of Roy Fisher in *City*, as he carefully avoids the center in a circumvention that suggests where the center might be.

The poems of the Pentecost sequence are brief: twelve short lines in each, divided into three stanzas. A number of the poems suggest two antiphonal voices. The short lines, mostly end-stopped, the rhymes and half rhymes, the repetitions and rhythms play their important parts. Meanings are brought up sharply at the ends of lines, giving them both an appearance of being definitive and a sense of directness, when in fact the poem is deliberately oblique:

> They slew by night
> upon the road

> Medina's pride
> Olmedo's flower.

The poems dwell on the speaker's relationship with Christ, on Christ's wounds and death, and on the wounds inflicted by Christ on the speaker. But these matters are removed from direct presentation: the desire to avoid possession of that which is desired, to elect the former terror of Yeats's alternatives in the epigraph, is a literary motive. Thus, the poem avoids engagement with its subjects by moving into various fictions. The opening poem, the first stanza of which is quoted above, is an example. The second poem is an allegory in the form of a medieval lyric:

> Down in the orchard
> I met my death
> under the briar rose
> I lie slain.

Most remarkable, however, in this tactic of artistic indirection is the removal of the subject matter into erotic terms in the manner practiced by St. John. From his prison cell, St. John heard a snatch of song from a street singer,

> I am dying of love,
> darling, what shall I do? [11]

and was inspired to use erotic idiom in his divine poems. So in Hill,

> This love will see me dead
> he has the place in mind
> where I am free to die
> be true at last true love

and

> Married and not for love ——
> you of all women

90

you of all women
my soul's darling my love.

St. John calls God *carillo*, darling.

The lowest stage of the speaker's relationship to Christ is arrived at in the seventh poem. Hill is again indebted to St. John, in particular to "Dark Night," the poem on which St. John wrote his lengthy commentaries, "The Ascent of Mt. Carmel" and "The Dark Night of the Soul"; Christ's darkness, because it is devastating in the privation of all earthly things, is the rich ground for the union of the soul with God:

Christ the deceiver
took all I had
his darkness ever
my fair reward.

Here is the beginning of an ascent, by lines with increasingly dominant rhymes, culminating in poem 13, in which paradoxes are triumphantly arrayed in lines rhyming or half rhyming in fours, with one notable exception.

Splendidly-shining darkness
proud citadel of meekness . . .
. . . .
and soul for soul discover
no strangeness to dissever
and lover keep with lover
a moment and for ever.

Thus go the beginning and the end of the poem, the rhymes providing an assertion so brazen as to arouse skepticism. The last two poems of the sequence return to the faltering conclusion that consummation of desire is an impossibility, though desire is the condition of this poetry. Yet in its ambiguity, the poem arrives at union: we do not know whether the words are the speaker's or Christ's:

I shall go down
to the lovers' well
and wash this wound
that will not heal

beloved soul
what shall you see
nothing at all
yet eye to eye

depths of non-being
perhaps too clear
my desire dying
as I desire.

We are attuned by this time to find that the "nothing" that is seen is everything and "non-being" fullness.

In the sequence "Lachrimae," the complex of retention and release is seen by Merle Brown as the paradox that "an essential quality of that which one can admire whole-heartedly is its being withheld."[12] The epigraph for the sequence is from Robert Southwell: "Passions I allow, and loves I approve, onely I would wish that men would alter their object and better their intent." The sequence dwells on the proper object of love, which is not the crucified body of Christ who, in the sixth sonnet, lives "unseen within that nakedness." The poet's distrust of his own love is expressed obliquely in overtones and puns throughout: "I pander to your name"; "self-love"; "clamorous love"; "I burn / to be enamoured"; "a passion amorous of my love." In the sequence, Hill is concerned also with the betrayal of the truth by ritual and art, as demonstrated in the last four lines of the sixth sonnet:

Triumphalism feasts on empty dread,
fulfilling triumphs of the festal year.

We find you wounded by the token spear.
Dominion is swallowed with your blood.

Brown comments that the poet's position is that "to take part in communion is to turn the truth into a saleable object, to swallow his Lord's blood is to swallow dominion"; "triumphalism" is the temptation "'of presenting the catastrophic course of events'—leading up to and away from the Crucifixion—'as expressive of the working of a traceable providential order.' The triumphalism of *Acts* indicates a succumbing to that temptation."[13]

Hill considers the rituals of art as an equivalent betrayal. In *Four Quartets*, T. S. Eliot turns in each fifth movement to the act of poetry, and the act is favored as an incarnation, analogous to *the* Incarnation, the embodiment that is the central mystery of the poem, as the Incarnation is the central mystery of Christianity. In some of the sestets of the "Lachrimae" sonnets, Hill similarly considers artifaction; but here it is a falsifying activity, self-flattering and self-nourishing, and its product is subject to decay. "I cannot turn aside from what I do," he confesses in the first sonnet. In the second, "self-love" is "the slavish master of this trade." The third presents a tapestry (in the octave here) as a grotesque fiction—"brooches of crimson tears where no eyes weep, / a mouth unstitched into a rimless cup"—the agent of expression, the mouth, has decayed in the decaying art work. In the octave of number 5, music's creation is a "fictive consonance"; in the sestet there is reproach in the idea of art: "Self-seeking hunter of forms, there is no end / to such pursuits." The sestet of the seventh sonnet opens, "So many nights the angel of my house / has fed such urgent comfort through a dream." The poem is a translation of a sonnet by Lope de Vega, but the comfort is a motif Hill has added. The octave has presented the speaker's unworthiness of Christ's assiduous attention.

The opening of the sestet suggests that the art in the poetry of the octave that has made the presentation has destroyed the thrust of the guilt and procured comfort, even as triumphalism similarly procures a sense of satisfaction in the fulfilment of design. Hill is yet another poet complaining of poiesis.

6

Ted Hughes

No other poet on either side of the Atlantic making a change of style in midcareer out of a sense of the infidelity and inadequacy of a traditional style has made changes as radical, as dramatic, and as costly as those of Ted Hughes. Author of two volumes of formal verse—*The Hawk in the Rain* and *Lupercal*—before the extraordinary appearances of *Wodwo* in 1967 and *Crow* in 1970, Hughes engages the attention partly because of the mastery of the formal style of his earlier verse, which he could use as naturally as language itself before he elected to write otherwise in *Wodwo* and even more so in *Crow* and in later poems. He has spoken of his stylistic change in an interview: "The idea [of *Crow*] was originally just to write . . . in a super-simple and a super-ugly language which would in a way shed everything except just what [Crow] wanted to say without any other consideration."[1] The style of *Crow* suggests that

---

Ted Hughes (b. 1930) was educated at Pembroke College, Cambridge. From the early volumes, *The Hawk in the Rain* and *Lupercal*, through *Wodwo* and *Crow*, to his most recent work, Hughes has remained among the most important figures in contemporary poetry. He took first prize in the 1958 Guinness Poetry Award, was named a Guggenheim Fellow for 1959–1960, received the Hawthornden Prize in 1961, was named to the Order of the British Empire in 1977, and received the Royal Society's Heinemann Bequest in 1980.

Hughes had had a Yeatsian vision of tomorrow's dispensation or had seen the writing and risen to leave the banquet: aware as a visionary of the age that is shortly to come, with the old familiar god and the pretty civilization destroyed, he wants to come to terms with a dehumanized postholocaust world; fearing what the new may bring, he prepares to meet it with a fearless style.[2] Or perhaps the new style responds rather to Hughes's increasing sense of the depth of human nature and to his awareness of the spirits who, in his words, "supply everything finally that we really want and need, and who once we have met them threaten to make our whole life seem trivial and false."[3] However the new style is to be attributed, traditional poetic forms are clearly insufficient. And traditional western rituals and mores are likewise insufficient to contain or harness the primal human energies operating behind the mask of civilization—the mask itself apparently disintegrating. After *Crow*, rather than familiar western experiences and the polite life of cities and domestic nature, Hughes's poetry increasingly embodies the conditions of Man, not men, and of psychic progressions like those described in records of the shaman. But even as he has putatively gone deeper into human nature, far beyond familiar human experiences and judgments into a world with its own new mythology, the writing in which these less accessible experiences are to be conveyed is itself obscure: communication is impaired.

There have been other changes: in *Orghast*,[4] Hughes sacrificed not only the traditional English poetic style but the English language itself; in *Season Songs*, the skill with the language and the poet's manifest delight in wielding it return in natural descriptions unapproached in this century. Later, the same skill is at work in the body of *Gaudete* and still later in much of *Moortown*; but in the epilogue of *Gaudete*, in parts of *Moortown*, and in *Cave Birds* still another style appears.

Hughes's early verse, formal, hewn rather than nicely chiselled, owes something to Richard Wilbur, whose influence Hughes acknowledges. He also acknowledges that of Shakespeare and John Crowe Ransom: from the latter he no doubt learned the management of a fable in a short poem, and the Reverend Bladderwrack's mighty performance among the whores in *The Burning of the Brothel* is clearly indebted to that of Ransom's Captain Carpenter in his military wars, who comes to mind again later in one or two other of Hughes's mutilated but indomitable figures. There is a good deal of animal poetry in the early volumes, in which animals are appealing, as they were to Marianne Moore, for their sincerity. They don't put on airs; they act according to instinct, of which the product is almost invariably energetic and most often violent. Several poems in *Lupercal*, for example, demonstrate Hughes's admiration for the singleness of purpose of the animals: the "coiled steel" of the thrush,[5] the horn of the bullfrog,[6] the lack of sophistry in the body of the hawk.[7] Like the animals, tramps and other primitive men belong to their own worlds, trust nature, and get on okay.

We are reminded of Marianne Moore (who, incidentally, was early in recognizing Hughes's talent) not only in the attitude toward animals in Hughes but in his use of detail and in his rhythms—features learned perhaps from Moore by Richard Wilbur, who is heard clearly in some of the rippling lines in the early volumes, such as these from "An Otter," another poem in *Lupercal*.

> Underwater eyes, an eel's
> Oil of water body, neither fish nor beast is the otter:
> Four-legged yet water-gifted, to outfish fish;
> With webbed feet and long ruddering tail
> And a round head like an old tomcat.

In contrast to the later flat and barren verse of *Crow*, "An Otter" shows how Hughes's early poems tend to be resonant and freighted with connotations from the heritage of the language:

> from sea
>
> To sea crosses in three nights
> Like a king in hiding. Crying to the old shape of the starlit land,
> Over sunken farms where the bats go round,
> Without answer. Till light and birdsong come
> Walloping up roads with the milk wagon.

The details of the poem bring to mind the dictum of David Jones, speaking in *The Anathémata* of the "efficient causes" of poetry, that poetry involves "squeezing every drain of evocation from the word-forms of the language. . . . And that involves a bagful of mythus before you've said Jack Robinson."

Animals are animals in Hughes, but often they possess human qualities. The bird in "Hawk Roosting," declaring, "My manners are tearing off heads," was accused by critics of being a Fascist, but Hughes said the bird only symbolized the violence in nature. His jaguar, in "The Jaguar," from *Hawk in the Rain*, was, he claimed, a "beautiful, powerful nature spirit, he is a homicidal maniac, he is a supercharged piece of cosmic machinery, he is a symbol of man's baser nature shoved down into the id and growing cannibal murderous with deprivation."[8]

The endemic energy and violence in nature account for the subject matter of many of the early poems. What is most interesting about the poems in *Hawk in the Rain*, however, is that the energy is generally controlled. For one thing, simply, many of the animals are in fact caged (Hughes has worked in a zoo); although imagination may release them, some limitation of their feral energy is achieved. In the jaguar, that energy is potential not kinetic: his "stride is wilderness of freedom" and "the world rolls under the long thrust of his heel," but the terrible power is within the control of the poet's imagination. There is deliberate control exerted by the two lovers of "Parlour-Piece," who, on account of the violence of their love,

> sat speechlessly:
> Pale cool tea in tea-cups chaperoned
> Stillness, silence, the eyes
> Where fire and flood strained.

"Secretary" begins with the thought, "If I should touch her she would shriek," but the speaker doesn't, and the woman goes to bed and "lies with buttocks tight / Hiding her lovely eyes until day break." In "Egg-Head," forgetfulness and madness are presented as protection from the monstrosities of the universe—"The whaled monstered sea-bottom, eagled peaks / And stars that hang over hurtling endlessness." In *Lupercal*, Hughes continued to present the strength of animals as curbed. "The Bull Moses," a massive animal, has his powers suppressed, and he is not enticed into action. The massive pig, in "View of a Pig," whose bite is worse than a horse's—"They chop a half-moon clean out," is dead. Even in "The Retired Colonel," the violence manifest is a thing of the past: "five or six wars / Stiffened in his reddened neck," that "man-eating British lion."

In addition to the presentation of energy subjugated, formal constraint in the verse renders the violence as humanly understood. In "Hawk Roosting," the bird that declares "My manners are tearing off heads," is uttering a silly bit of canned and calculated ugliness; but it is set, nonetheless, in a context of which the imposed form persuades us—obliquely, to be sure—that it is all right: the universe can contain such a note as part of its harmony; nature can combine violence with its benefits. In "An Otter," for instance, water both nourishes the otter and drowns it; the air is "tainted and necessary"; and the land gives him "his length and the mouth of the hound." The whole style of "Hawk Roosting" sanctions the hawk's remark: "It took the whole of Creation / To produce my foot, my each feather." The animal and its behavior are part of the design of the world; in the style there is the familiar measured rhythm, the syntactical order, and diction that appeals to the tradition with its associations and connections. As in other poems of Hughes's early work, there is the sense that pain is meaningful, like that which occurs in tragedy as part of a larger purpose or that which brought Eliot's Philomel to fill "all the desert with inviolable voice."

In the matter of violence, Hughes claims to differ from the Movement poets: they had been in the war, he points out, and had had enough of rhetoric, power, and heroic efforts; the war had "set them dead against negotiation with anything outside the cosiest arrangement of society. They wanted it cosy. . . . I came a bit later. I hadn't had enough. I was all for opening negotiations with whatever happened to be out there."[9] His early poems speak to native cruelty—"man's baser nature shoved down." There is not, however, any direct comment in his poems on the grim inhumanity in Western Europe that has engaged George Steiner so intensely, who has remarked that "a man can read Goethe or Rilke in the evening . . . can play Bach or Schubert, and go to his day's work at Auschwitz in the morning."[10] But Hughes is profoundly aware of the gap that exists between what he considers real life and much contemporary art and poetry. In his introduction to the poems of Vasko Popa, speaking of him and his contemporaries, Hughes says their poetry

> seems closer to the common reality, in which we have to live if we are to survive, than to those other realities in which we can holiday, or into which we decay when our bodily survival is comfortably taken care of, and which art, particularly con-

temporary art, is forever trying to impose on us as some sort of superior dimension. I think it was Miłosz, the Polish poet, who when he lay in a doorway and watched the bullets lifting the cobbles out of the street beside him realized that most poetry is not equipped for life in a world where people actually do die. But some is. And the poets of whom Popa is one seem to have put their poetry to a similar test.[11]

Hughes's attempts to equip his poetry similarly have not been universally accepted. Whereas A. Alvarez calls Hughes one of "the select band of survivor-poets whose work is adequate to the destructive reality we inhabit," John Bayley calls this "fashionable nonsense." Reviewing *Gaudete*, a later work by Hughes, he adds, "This is poetry suited to a tepid, coddled, welfare society, dreaming of violence in front of the television screen, which is projecting its immaculate coloured details, blood or sunburn, wildlife or underwater, superbly shot by telephoto lens."[12]

The experiences of the figures in Hughes's work may reflect the processes of initiation and the rites and spectacles of shamanism. These, Hughes says, are as ubiquitous in life as if they had biological rather than cultural grounds,[13] and they appear in protean forms, generally less directly than in his own work, in much Western poetry. Indeed, in all his work, the later especially, readers may find such elements of shamanism as dismemberment and death, cleansing and renewal, ascent to the sky and descent to the underworld. When the early work is compared with the later, a new moral attitude toward an existence fraught with pain is apparent. In the former, we are presented most often with the animals that are agents of violence and cruelty; in the latter, we get more of the victims. Often, however, agent and victim are one and the same. In *Wodwo*, the poems, the short stories, and the radio play are all to be read together, the poet instructs us in the author's note, as complementary parts of a single work. In this volume, unlike *The Hawk in the Rain* and *Lupercal*, the acceptance of pain is a pervading theme. If, as has been suggested, Hughes's animals bring clairvoyant information from the spirit world,[14] the message is of man's identity with nature, painful as it may be, and of his proper obedience to that pain. Pain accepted apparently leads to power; pain repudiated, to weakness.

Thus, in the first story in *Wodwo*, "The Rain Horse," the young man returning to the farm had expected something, "some pleasure, some meaningful sensation"[15]; but when it comes—comes *at* him, in fact—in the form of a marauding horse, he doesn't recognize it. He stones it and drives it away. Then, however, he is almost overcome with weakness: he "fought to keep his breath"; "making an effort, he heaved his weight over the gate-top." He experiences a pain in the chest and feels in the end as if "some important part had been cut out of his brain."[16] In "Sunday," the second story, in the hot cobbled yard of a country pub, a boy witnesses the act of Billy Red—who grabs a rat in his teeth and shakes it to death.[17] The boy is nauseated, and the pain in his head may be read, in the light of the previous story, as a result of his inability to identify with violence in nature. However, the act of catching animals with the teeth, indicating transformation into a wild animal, is part of the initiatory rites of a shaman candidate, when he has withdrawn into the wilderness, and the travesty performed by Billy Red in "Sunday" is an example of the substitution, of which there is more in *Crow*, of a primitive ritual for Western conventions. There are similar matters afoot in "The Harvesting," in which Mr. Grooby, shooting the game at the cutting field, is out of touch with nature, longing for his car and the smell of the cool upholstery; each time he fires at the hare, he is himself stunned.[18] (The motif of injury reflected onto its agent is repeated in

Crow.) *The Wound*, the radio play, is the nightmare fantasy of a soldier in the Second World War. During a long hallucination, he is led through surreal scenes and situations; once again, in the journey through the dead land, the river they cross, the chateau they come to and its lady, the meals—all are elements belonging to one or another of the rituals of shamanism. Finally, when the point of view shifts at the end, we learn that the soldier has been shot through the head, though not killed. Most details of the play need not detain us, but it is worth noticing that in two places the soldier seems momentarily to sink out of his hallucination into reality and, when he does so, he records his presence, his headache, and power: "Me. Ripley, in power. With a headache," in one place; in another, "We're here. Good old Ripley. In power. With a headache."[19]

Two small notes in a long reverie, but they are echoed and elaborated later in the volume in "The Song of a Rat," a poem in three parts that embodies a statement about pain that again looks forward to *Crow*. The poem announces first that the rat is in the trap, screeching, defying the universe that has injured it, but then, the rat seems suddenly to understand. "It bows and is still, / With a little beseeching of blood on its nose-end." After the understanding, it enters into a visionary experience: part 2, "The Rat's Vision." Finally, in the third part, "The Rat's Flight," the rat crosses "into power." In "The Howling of Wolves," "steel traps" are presented ambiguously as the agents of both the wolves and their foes; the wolf howls, but it is not certain "whether out of agony or joy." Both poems were written in the month of Sylvia Plath's suicide.[20]

The acceptance of suffering is the duty also of the skylarks in the poem "Skylarks." They too are in the trap of nature, obedient and committed, and it is apt enough in the poet's vision as demonstrated elsewhere in *Wodwo* that their singing should be conceived of as pain, "the whole agony," though at the same time it is pain pervaded by a sense of duty and satisfaction, the birds themselves being both agents and victims.

> Crueller than owl or eagle
>
> A towered bird, shot through the crested head
> With the command, Not die
> But climb
>
> Climb
>
> Sing
>
> Obedient as to death a dead thing.

The rituals of pain, once again, are enacted on a Sunday.

The poems in *Wodwo* are in a freer verse than Hughes had previously used. And there is less rhetoric. There is some obscurity, due, one may say, to the fallibility of the human medium for perceiving and interpreting the mysteries of the world, in which the acceptance of pain brings about spiritual gain.

In most of the poems of *Crow* there is no mystery at all: everything is clear; denotations are patent, connotations absent. What Hughes calls the "terrible, suffocating, maternal octopus of ancient English poetic tradition,"[21] which had so munificently fostered his early verse, has been largely avoided; the language in most of these poems has no ghosts, but it is ugly and flat; there are few adjectives (though black appears quite often); sentences are predominately simple or compound, rarely complex. Although some of the poems are in regular meter, traditional verse forms have, for the most part, been jettisoned, along with the myths that have fed our sense of order from time immemorial and have protected our sleep. There are mythic parallels and allusions, inversions, and parodies, but Hughes's concern was to produce something with the minimal cultural accretions of the museum sort—something autochthonous and complete in itself, as it might be invented after the holocaust and demolition of all libraries, where essential things spring again—if at all—only from their seeds in nature—and are not lugged around or hoarded as preserved harvests from the past. So the comparative religion/mythology background was irrelevant to me, except as I could forget it. If I couldn't find it again original in Crow, I wasn't interested to make a trophy of it.[22]

Among the *Crow* poems, there is a repeated belittlement or an ironic glance at the orders and forms that constitute the way of life in the West. Like other examples of contemporary literature, following the endlessly disturbing wake of Freud, Frazer, and the physicists of the first decade in the twentieth century, the *Crow* poems speak to the insufficiency of the power of Western rationalism and its products. The title of one, "The Battle of Osfrontalis," might stand for one of the major debates in contemporary culture, the battle between primitivism and sophisticated intellection, joined early, for instance, by D. H. Lawrence and others, when Westerners began to perceive the wisdom and power of Africa and Asia, no longer limiting themselves to European culture and tradition. In "The Battle of Osfrontalis," Crow stands firm against words that mount their onslaught with curious fragments from our civilization—life insurance policies, warrants, blank checks, and some surrealistic curiosities. Words, Hughes believed, being stronger than the raw life of our experience can and do displace it.[23] The poem is characteristic of others in the volume, in that it proceeds by action and response. Then, except that they provide the overall sense that Crow finally defeats words, the images are inconsequential; they are merely words, energetic and shocking, otherwise almost completely unimportant in their reference. Nor do the proper nouns and allusions enrich meaning; like the other images they might as well be interchanged.

> Words came with blank cheques—
> He drew Minnie Mice on them.
> Words came with Aladdin's lamp—
> He sold it and bought a pie.
> Words came in the likeness of vaginas in a row—
> He called in his friends.
> Words came in the likeness of a wreathed vagina pouring
>   out Handel—
> He gave it to the museum.

An allusion to *Hamlet*,

> Words retreated, suddenly afraid
> Into the skull of a dead jester,

does not provide the depth of meaning that it would, say, in a poem by Eliot or Geoffrey Hill: the associations of "poor Yorick" cannot be clearly related. The allusion does, however, create a memory of the old, lost human condition, which, as will appear, rears up nostalgically on occasion in these poems.

Words appear again in "A Disaster" where Crow sees language killing men, bulldozing cities to ruin, and poisoning seas. We are reminded of "the Word," that for Henri Chopin has "created profit, it has justified work, it has made obligatory the confusion of occupation (to be doing something), it has permitted life to lie. The Word has become incarnate in the Vatican, on the rostrums of Peking, at the Elysée, etc."[24] In another poem, on the other hand, "Crow Goes Hunting," words are apparently on Crow's side, as he uses them for miscellaneous acts of destruction until they are eaten by the hare. In "Crow's Account of St. George," Crow is attacked by the patron saint of England, who stands here for the institution of numbers, the means of counting, against which primitive communities maintained a strong taboo. As champion of numbers, however, St. George stands also for the Western world of calculation, logic, and measurement—mental processes that have distinguished our minds since Plato and insulated us, maybe, from the sense of the being of things. In "Revenge Fable," a man attacks his mother, his primitive source perhaps, with "numbers and equations and laws / Which he invented and called truth."

It has been pointed out that poems in *Crow* demonstrate the inability of our habitual methods, including Christian rituals, to control the primitive energies of the world.[25] Crow, for example, participates in the Communion service in "Crow Communes" by tearing off and swallowing a mouthful of God. Christianity for Hughes has been designated by Keith Sagar as "just another provisional myth,"[26] and thus for other Christian traditions Crow substitutes non-Western or homemade alternatives—the Talmudic version of the creation in "A Childish Prank," for example; and, among other revisions, there is a farcical version of the Eden myth in "Apple Tragedy."

The loss of faith in Western rationalism may be reflected in the general absence in *Crow* of regular verse forms, which also belong to calculation and measurement. Hughes has observed: "When the old rituals and dogma have lost credit and disintegrated, and no new ones have been formed, the energy cannot be contained";[27] among the "old rituals" may be the traditional poetic ones. These again may be included in or be an index of civilization, the complete disappearance of which Hughes recognizes, as we have seen, as more than a mere possibility.[28] The question as to the cause of the change in his style might be answered somewhat glibly: no order in nature, no order in the verse. The absence of form in verse that describes a matter-of-fact naturalism may remind us of a comment by

John Crowe Ransom on Hardy's "Satires of Circumstance":
"In formal verse they contradict all our presumptions as to
this art, inasmuch as we have felt that poetry cannot consist with a naturalism both malignant and matter-of-fact,
to which no voice opposes itself with any prospect of escape."[29] Accordingly, one might say in connection with
Crow that such naturalism could not be consistent with
formal poetry.

In relinquishing the traditional verse forms and the he-
reditary wealth of the language that had earlier served him
so well, Hughes may have considered that the control they
provided for the natural energies in his verse precluded
him from coming at the world as he was seeing it, as he
believes Vasko Popa did. The lack of structure in *Crow* is
not absolute. We can interpret the poems and discover in
them subjects, themes, and motifs. But they have, all the
same, a most miscellaneous texture and an arbitrariness
approaching the surreal in the details presented; Hughes
is indebted here, it appears, to techniques in some of Popa's
early poems. The quality the two poets have in common is
an uneasy association of extravagance, apparently surrealistic, with a perfect simplicity of action and clarity of style
that momentarily disguises the terrible things going on. In
Popa's poems, as in *Crow*, activities that have a curious
kind of bloodless horror about them are often rendered as
games. Indeed, there is a series titled "Games," of which
one poem, "The Nail," opens,

> One be the nail another the pincers
> The other are workmen.

The pincers try to get the nail out of the ceiling:

> Usually they only pull his head off
> . . . .
> Then the workmen say

The pincers are no good
They smash their jaws and break their arms
And throw them out of the window.

The resemblances with *Crow* are particularly strong in a series called "The Quartz Pebble." Another game, depicted in "The Heart of the Quartz Pebble," shows how "they" played with the pebble, smashed it, opened its heart, and roused the snake coiled there.

They looked from afar
The snake coiled round the horizon
Swallowed it like an egg

—a trick similar to those in Crow's repertoire. In another poem of the series, "The Secret of the Quartz Pebble," the pebble has "filled himself with himself":

Has he eaten too much of his own tough flesh
Does he feel ill
. . . . . .
Is he pregnant perhaps
Will he give birth to a stone
Or to a wild beast or a streak of lightning

Ask him as much as you like
Don't expect an answer

Expect only a bump
Or a second nose or a third eye
Or who knows what.

In "Horse," there is the following figure, outrageous but easily matched by extravagancies in *Crow.*

Usually
He has eight legs

Between his jaws
Man came to live
From his four corners of earth
Then he bit his lips to blood

He wanted
To chew through that maize stalk.

Limited as it is, this sampling adequately demonstrates an affinity between works that in their quietly horrid manner may be said to come at the real world as, in Hughes's claim, Vasko Popa found it.

We must, however, go beyond the source in Popa and the concept of *Crow* as a concern with the inability of Western practices to control energy. Like some of the earlier animals in Hughes's menagerie, Crow is both the agent and the victim of a great deal of pain. He suffers assault and battery, to an enormous degree: hammered, burned, blasted, torn apart, he sustains Promethean injuries or, what are in fact greater, injuries such as those inflicted upon television cartoon characters that regularly bounce up again after having been demolished by incredible blows.[30] In "Crow's Last Stand," there was one thing "The sun could not burn," Crow's eye. In "Crow's Battle Fury," the injured animal is reconstituted with odd bits of borrowed anatomy:

> (With his glared off face glued back into position
> A dead man's eyes plugged back into his sockets
> A dead man's heart screwed in under his ribs
> His tattered guts stitched back into position
> His shattered brains covered with a steel cowl)
>
> He comes forward a step,
>   and a step,
>   and a step.

Suffering and reconditioned, like Ransom's Captain Carpenter, victim of the violence of experience but stupidly recovering, Crow becomes a model, like the rat and the skylark, for the new attitude toward painful existence. At his own and others' suffering, he laughs. Or, with even greater insouciance, faced with monumental pain or unlimited destruction, he turns to and commences to eat:

when he saw the word bulldozing whole cities to rubble,
"he ate well";[31] when

> the only face left in the world
> Lay broken . . .
> Crow had to start searching for something to eat.[32]

In a moment of utter hopelessness, when even "God went off in despair," Crow's response is active and instinctive; he "stropped his beak and started in on the two thieves."[33] A comment on the work of Popa and his crowd is again apt. "In a way," says Hughes, "their world reminds one of Beckett's world. Only theirs seems braver, more human, and so more real. It is as horrible as his, but they do not despair of it to the point of surrendering consciousness and responsibility to their animal cells. Their poetic themes revolve around the living suffering spirit, capable of happiness, much deluded, too frail, with doubtful and provisional senses, so undefinable as to be almost silly, but palpably existing, and wanting to go on existing—and this is not, as in Beckett's world, absurd."[34] The toughness that doesn't despair is likewise a quality of Crow's. If the poems inherit from the earlier books the theme of pain, there is here a remarkable intensification: Crow inflicts pain and endures it; he laughs uproariously and gorges.

The poems for the most part are in a flat language, from which human significance has largely been drained. They reflect, often, the basic conditions of life from which most of us do not wish to forfeit our traditional insulation. This is not altogether the case, however: the human voice and the world of human values are not absolutely lost. There are the traditional passages of verse in which the ghostly language of heritage and the presence of a human sensibility may occasionally be detected, as if a committed stoic should entertain an atrophied longing for grace, which does not diminish but enhances the overall sense of despair. There are fragments that suggest an older poetry, a slight mystery, human values, and even a little majesty: "A Horrible Religious Error," for example, refers to "the rustling of the spheres"; in "Crow's Vanity," there is reference to "misty ballerinas" and "hanging gardens." There is a touch here, perhaps, of Wallace Stevens, in the imprecise images, and again in "Dawn's Rose," in which a cry is as wordless as a gunshot and its "after-rale." There are the occasional interspersed references to those parts of nature that, unlike much in *Crow*, are not finally burned out and damned: "You are beautiful," says the hyena to the elephant in "Crow's Elephant Totem Song":

> We envy your grace
> Waltzing through the thorny growth
> O take us with you to the Land of Peaceful
> O ageless eyes, of innocence and kindliness.

Then in two poems that relate to the sea, Hughes expresses a central sense of loss. In one, "Crow and the Sea," Crow tries to relate to the sea: he tries ignoring it, talking to it; he tries sympathy and hate—all in vain.

> Finally
>
> He turned his back and he marched away from the sea
>
> As a crucified man cannot move.

In the other, "Crow on the Beach," Crow is again frustrated, because he grasps something of the sea's mystery but lacks the brains to understand its outcry. In "Crow's Playmates," Crow can be lonely, and in "Crow's Nerve Fails," he can bear a sense of sin: because "He cannot be forgiven," he flies "Heavily." The volume is thoroughly heterogeneous, and the texture varies. Indeed, even though he may hope, as Peter Dale suggests, that "the nifty reader will make connexions for himself,"[35] there is no certainty that Hughes intends the contents to be a unity rather than a mere collection of poems. He has said that they are linked together by a fable—but this, in our case, we do not have.[36] It is possible, however, that he intends to remind us fairly frequently that Crow, although no longer human, once was.

Most of the poems, however, have dispensed with such humanistic depth and proceed often by quick parallel clauses in which the human is confused with technology and causes produce illogical effects, such as occur in "Crow's Song of Himself."

> When God hammered Crow
> He made gold
> When God roasted Crow in the sun
> He made diamond
> When God crushed Crow under weights
> He made alcohol.

Hughes had used the style earlier in *Scapegoats and Rabies: A Poem in Five Parts*, in which the soldiers get

> Their heroic loom
> From the statue stare of old women,
> From the trembling chins of old men,
> From the napes and bow legs of toddlers,
> From the absolute steel
> Of their automatic rifles. . . .

The world vision of the early poems that was akin to tragedy has given way to one closer to comedy or farce. Suffering is not handled in the high Greek manner. Perhaps it shouldn't be: in the aesthetic universe, says Herbert Marcuse, "joy and fulfillment find their proper place alongside pain and death. . . . The terror and the pleasure of reality are purified. But the achievement is illusory, false, fictitious: it remains within the dimension of art, a work of art; in reality fear and frustration go on unabated."[37]

In *Crow* suffering becomes routine. Throughout the book and through all the horrendous destruction, images repeatedly work to eliminate the distinction between mechanical and natural and between human and nonhuman: trees cough; tears are nickel plated; Crow has rubber eyes and clockwork ears; the earth has a sump outlet and has shrunk to the size of a hand grenade; Crow unites heaven and earth with nails; he has an electrode in his brain. Human feelings are starved out, as in "Crow's Account of the Battle," which relegates horror to insignificance.

This had happened too often before
. . . .
Bones were too like lath and twigs
Blood was too like water
. . . . . .
And shooting somebody through the midriff
Too like potting a snooker ball
Too like tearing up a bill
Blasting the whole world to bits
Was too like slamming a door.

With the flat, matter-of-fact style, with such juxtapositions, and amid the crass insouciance at the impossible sufferings, many of the *Crow* poems seem divested of any human association, and no familiarly accepted values preside. They recall, as one reflects upon the volume as a whole, a comment of Leo Steinberg's about *Target with Faces*, a painting by Jasper Johns: "A dismembered face, multiplied, blinded, repeats four times above the impersonal stare of a bull's-eye. Bull's-eye and blind faces—but juxtaposed as if by habit or accident, without any expressive intent. As if the values that would make a face seem more precious or eloquent or remarkable had ceased to exist; as if those who could hold and impose such values just weren't around."[38] The response to *Crow* on the part of many readers may well be that of a New York painter quoted by Steinberg, who remarked on seeing Johns's painting, "Well, I am still involved with the dream." But perhaps the cartoon-based art of Roy Lichtenstein or other pop artists supplies a closer parallel than Johns's, and Lichtenstein's much-quoted comment is apt: "Pop art looks out into the world; it appears to accept its environment, which is not good or bad, but different, another state of mind."

There are resemblances in Crow's behavior to that attributed to various gods in primitive religions: the creation by naming, for example; the reification of words; the hacking up of bodies; cannibalism; and so on. No doubt primitive people conceive of such gods so that by propitiating a figure associated with cruelty they may provide some kind of acceptable framework for it and appease their terrors. So Hughes may be considered in *Crow* to be placating what appalls him in the world, fictitiously locating and embodying the cruel forces. But Crow, of course, is victim as well as perpetrator of cruelty. Managing his despair by sheer physical effrontery, hardened against it by his own dehumanization, he is efficiently equipped to accept the pain in the universe, following the principle that gains an increasingly manifest importance throughout Hughes's poems.

Crow, Hughes says, is created by "God's nightmare's attempt to improve on man."[39] And he is certainly an improvement—if adaptation to environment is the main criterion in such judgments and if the world is in fact as burned out as it most often appears in these poems. He is an improvement because he sides with nature, identifying with those forces in the universe that, since midcentury, we need never hope again to tame or even understand. Hughes's development has led to a point at which the acceptance of pain in a painful universe becomes an increasingly significant obligation. But whereas in the earlier poetry pain was part of a humanly understood order, in *Crow* the sense of human order and human feeling has atrophied, and the fulgurations of its aftershine illuminate only a barren scenario in which pain, abundant enough, is without a context and not to be understood, a desert that no nightingale fills with inviolable voice. That most of the verse lacks form may be attributed to the loss of faith in the efficacy of the human power to order: Crow responds to the pain of an amoral universe with raucous laughter; Hughes relinquishes the traditional controls of poetic diction, form, logical context—impositions appropriate only to a world tamed to human proportions. He rules out tensions and forfeits opportunities for any other tone than that of flat, straightforward description. The poet's gift is an "unobliging thing," Hughes says: "Certain memories, images, sounds, feelings, thoughts, and relationships between these, have for some reason become luminous at the core of his mind: it is in his attempt to bring them out, without impairment, into a comparatively dark world that he makes poems. At the moment of writing, the poetry is a combination, or a resultant, of all that he is, unimpeachable evidence of itself and, indirectly, of himself, and for the time of writing he can do nothing but accept it."[40] In the late sixties, the gift led Hughes to *Crow*, in which the protagonist fights against words and the poet rejects literary tradition for "super-ugly language." Then, unsatisfied by this divestment, he breaks away from the language altogether, using for the play *Orghast*, presented in Persia, an invented language; he did so, he says, to avoid the "haphazard associations of English, which continually tries to supplant experience and truth with the mechanisms of its own autonomous life." Thus, along with Greek and Persian, there is Hughes's own language, Orghast, in which light is *hoan* and dark *bullorga* and the *Kr* sound means devour. What he was looking for, he said, was "mainly a way of hanging together musical moments, rather than a dramatic plot. The point was to create a precise but open and inviting language, inviting to a lost world we wanted to explore. Music is one such language—mathematically precise, but completely mysterious and open, giving access to a deeper world, closed to direct analysis."[41]

His next move might well have been to silence, where others before him, in what seems a dilemma of the same category, had in their own ways proceeded. The art of our time, says Susan Sontag, "is noisy with appeals for silence."[42] He returns to the English language, however, in *Prometheus on His Crag*, a sequence of twenty-one short poems in which he rewrites the myth of Prometheus and his ordeal. But Hughes still discredits words; in the nineteenth poem, in which Prometheus invents language,

> speech starts hopefully to hold
> Pieces of the wordy earth together
> But pops to space-silence and space-cold.
> . . . .
> And the mouth shuts
> Savagely on a mouthful
> Of space-fright which makes the ears ring.

Words in this poem are identified with birds, which, in an earlier poem of the sequence (number 3), are victims of a variant of the Fall: the woodpecker "Howled laughter into dead holes. / The birds became what birds have ever since been."

The sequence begins, as *Crow*, with the creation of the protagonist and proceeds immediately to his unconscious acceptance of suffering, leading him to feel his strength. He asserted his existence with "a world's end shout" that brought about the condition like the Fall and "woke the vulture." New pain ensues. Yet in number 10, Prometheus comes to accept it by admiring its source, the vulture, which in turn accepts its own pain.

> It knew what it was doing
> . . . .
> Balancing the gift of life
>
> And the cost of the gift
> Without a tremor—
> As if both were nothing.

Prometheus learns to recognize himself as suffering at the center of every aeon "like the grit in its pearl." The sixteenth poem shows him becoming, like Christ, the agent of atonement:

> He lays himself down in his chains
> On the Mountain,
>   under Heaven
>   as THE PAYMENT
> Too far from his people to tell them
>
> Now they owe nothing.

In *Season Songs*, Hughes returns to something of his earlier style. The volume contains twenty-four poems interleaved with sixteen pictures by Leonard Baskin (not in the style of the cartoons that illuminated *Crow*), depicting some of the natural scenes of the four seasons that the poems describe. The pictures are mostly watercolors, vivid, representative of the central features and modishly vague in the backgrounds. The scenes described in the poems are chronologically ordered, beginning in March with a newborn calf and running to the dead, frozen end of the year. Some of the poems are of individual animals and some of familiar features of the seasons in general.

Hughes's superb descriptions of nature are unapproached by others in this century. His relentless power to press words into descriptive service is remarkable even while he pretends to despair of their efficacy. Getting into words the world of the crow's wingbeat is impossible, he says: "the ominous thing in the crow's flight, the barefaced, bandit thing, the battered beggarly gipsy thing, the caressing and shaping yet slightly clumsy gesture of the downstroke, as if the wings were both too heavy and too powerful, and the headlong sort of merriment, the macabre pantomime ghoulishness and the undertaker sleekness."[43] You could say all this, he believes, and still fail.

Season Songs is intended primarily for children, but the poems are not softly incognizant of the danger and suffering in a world where bullets lift cobblestones from the street and poets cower. Again, into many of the poems of this volume, especially into those in which the scene is predominantly halcyon, pain is deliberately introduced. In "A March Calf," for instance, the poet notes amid descriptive lines about this "dear little fellow" that butchers are developing expertise and markets. Pain, danger, and grief are frequently introduced at the ends of poems: the hunted stag weeps at the end of "The Stag"; "Swifts" closes with a description of one that is crippled and dies; "Hay" closes with a hint of the destruction of innocence; "Sheep" ends in anguish. There is much in this volume reminiscent of D. H. Lawrence—the poem about the calf, for example, shows both the accuracy of description and the patronizing tone of *Birds, Beasts and Flowers*:

> Right from the start he is dressed in his best—his black
>   and his whites.
> Little Fauntleroy—quiffed and glossy,
> A Sunday suit, a wedding natty get-up.

Hughes has not in these poems returned exclusively to the style of his earliest volumes, which manifest the human perspective in the formal structure. There are occasional passages reminiscent of *Crow*, as he apparently sets off with a formula that may carry him where it will, and random similes are bound together by a tight rhythm and rhyme as in this passage from "The Warm and the Cold":

> But the trout is in its hole
> Like a chuckle in a sleeper.
> The hare strays down the highway
> Like a root going deeper.

But for much of the volume, the poet is very much in control—seeing the natural world from a perspective familiar to tradition, sustaining the tradition with his individual panache.

Gaudete tells in prose and free verse the story of the Reverend Nicholas Lumb, an Anglican clergyman. The "Argument" tells us that the real Mr. Lumb has been carried away by spirits for an unnamed purpose and replaced by a figure made out of a log in his exact likeness. This version of Lumb, intending to produce a new Messiah, has seduced the women of the parish. The setting is the stylized English rural parish that appears, for example, in an Agatha Christie novel, containing one each of the several species often found in reality in such communities—the farmer, the retired army major, the poacher, the publican, the eccentric, their wives. The prologue describes the surreal experiences that constitute the initiation of the real Lumb into his unusual duties and the creation from a tree of his surrogate. The experiences are reminiscent of those endured by a character, Morgan, at the end of *Eat Crow*, a play by Hughes, published in 1971, who is apparently undergoing some mortifying ritual after having encountered his double, Morgantwo. In *Gaudete* we are not always clear as to which Lumb is which. The central part of the book presents in separate sections, each from the point of view of one of the parishioners, one day, the pseudoLumb's last, in the life of the parish. In one section in the middle of the book, Lumb is subjected to some primitive rituals in which, crawling in mire, he is beaten and trampled by cattle; there he encounters a female figure whom he first tries to save but from whom he later fights to free himself. In another section, Lumb rescues a girl from his double who has mysteriously emerged like a monster from the sea. Most of the book, however, is given to the description in rich, concrete images of the characters, their occupations, and their discovery of Lumb's activities. Much of it comes on in one of Hughes's characteristic styles—in perceptive, metaphorical, violent language in long lines or in prose. Following a shot, "the long carpet of echoes unrolls / Across the still land into the upholstered distance";[44] in the morning, "Giant wheels of light ride into the chestnuts";[45] a man whose daughter has committed suicide is "looking right through the photograph to his unburied daughter and the stump-raw amputation of that morning's event."[46]

The epilogue is a group of some forty short poems, hymns, and psalms "to a nameless female deity," the figure with whom the pseudoLumb had engaged in the ritual mentioned above. The poems are composed, according to a note, by the real Lumb. They are in the first person, addressing the deity, describing the violence, pain, and destruction that the speaker has experienced and that are part of the ritual means of entry into unity with the not infallible goddess, who repeatedly reveals and veils herself. The burden of the poems is not entirely clear—Mr. Lumb, John Bayley notes, is not so good a poet as Hughes;[47] the "precision" that Bayley claims for the style (he is quoted on the book jacket) is not easily measured in the epilogue when what is being described is quite foreign to most human experience. It is apparently intended, nonetheless, that the story of Lumb and his women devotees in *Gaudete* proper is an allegory, a related play; the epilogue describes the real thing, which itself, of course, as a spiritual experience, can only come into language in some form of metaphor or other.

The epilogue has no sustained pattern. Except for a passage or two referring to Lumb's previous experience with the female deity, the individual poems are efforts to embody an act in the ritual: images of birth appear toward the beginning; the speaker then seeks to identify with the earth, then to submerge the ego and identify with "her" kingdom. "She" is all things: all nature is the pressure of her footfall. But the language for the most part resists translation into meaning.

Cave Birds is written in the same style, which, with occasional reversions, has progressively developed away from the vivid concretion and conventional structure of the early work, even as the realms of magic and unreason have called for the tortuous reconstruction of the earlier language based on sense and logic. *Cave Birds* appeared first in the limited Scolar Press edition of 1975, which presented ten poems selected from a sequence of twenty written by Hughes to accompany the drawings of Leonard Baskin. With each of the ten is the drawing to which the poem was written, as well as the reproduction of a selected working paper, mostly in appalling handwriting, one embellished with coffee stains. The paper is handmade in Amalfi and the edition, unbound, is boxed and about three feet long. The Baskin drawings represent owls, crows, a pelican, an osprey, a rooster, a swift, and an eagle, occasionally unfleshed and always unnatural, with added, exaggerated, and distorted features.

The book is a mythology. Except in the first poem, the birds superintend a progression engaged in by a character addressed as "you," and the progression seems to consist of the poet-mortal experiences of a soul—death and destruction leading to regeneration and birth. Edwin Morgan notes, "That the *drama* of the sequence is largely a drama of dying, judgment, afterlife, and rebirth suggests the old Hermes/Thoth identification and the Ancient Egyptian religious rituals, both of the weighing of souls and of the continuance of life."[48] The first poem, "The Knight," describes the quester himself in the third person; and the drawing has a rough relationship to the words. The extent to which each poem is related to its drawing varies: a poem may begin in some recognizable description then move away in its own evolution. Close relationship could hardly be maintained when the abstract and surrealistic imagery in all the poems leads away from any visual identifications.

The themes of the poems are suggested rather than clearly stated. The series begins with the absolutes of destruction, "skylines tear him apart, winds drink him." The second poem suggests alleviation of pain. In the third come annihilation and judgment: the drawing shows a crow crouched in an egg, "awaiting judgement in after life"; the poem ends with the speaker's "soul-skin laid out / A mat for my judges." Number 4 presents the interrogation, instant conviction, and sentence by "Death's Doorway Guard"; the drawing, a two-headed osprey. Next, there is the suggestion of comfort, the drawing showing an owl, presiding and seductively reassuring, the lines unusually lacking in violence, but suggesting duplicity:

> This earth is heaven's sweetness
> It is heaven's mother.
> . . . .
> You shall see
> How tenderly she has wiped her child's face clean.
> Of the bitumen of blood and the smoke of tears.

Threatening and punishment in the sixth poem lead to sensualism and frivolity in number 7, the drawing for the latter presenting a flamboyant cockerel, the lines wild and the meaning more than usually inaccessible.

The frilled lizard of cavort
Ran in his wheel like a man, burned by breath.

The baboon of panoply
Jumped at the sky-rump of a greasy rainbow

The flag of the crotch, his glistenings tapered to touch.

There is ascetic reduction in number 8, as the drawing, "The True Guide," depicts a swift—emaciated, hunched, arms and legs akimbo, as if crucified on a barn door—but the opening lines suggest the beginning of redemption: "When everything that can fall has fallen / Something rises." Next, there is regeneration, with a drawing of a bare crow impaled like Saint Sebastian with quills, the lines beginning, "What is left is just what my life bought me: / the gem of myself," coming later to,

Movement is still patient with me—
Lightness beyond lightness releasing me further.
And the mountains of torment and mica

Pass me by.

Finally come a drawing of an owl called "the angel with good news," a huge sphere of feathers, and lines describing new life. What Keith Sagar says of *Prometheus on His Crag*, a sequence that Hughes calls "a limbo . . . a numb poem about numbness," might also be said of the epilogue to *Gaudete* and of *Cave Birds*: "The poems are the stages of the psychic journey subjectively experienced, objectified as myth."[49] The Faber and Faber edition of 1978 contains twenty-eight poems with drawings by Baskin on the facing pages. It is subtitled *An Alchemical Cave Drama*. Poems and pictures have been added to the limited edition and the shadowy paradigm of the postmortal progression from death to birth is further embellished. There are additional birds playing the parts of judge, executioner, false comforter, and there are additional poems expressing guilt and oppression and poems in which humanoids are put together with mechanical parts, reminiscent of the confusion of nature and technology in *Crow*.

For most of the volume the texture of the poems consists of mixed metaphor, paradox, and heterogeneous ideas yoked by violence together. Crow, in his sequence, moved around a world that although phantasmagoric was one that could be visualized inasmuch as it took solid features from our own: if there were things that we could neither visualize nor conceive of, such as the "blanks between stars" and the "deafness of the gulf," there were solid counters like the rain-sodden shoe, the garbage can, the dropped ice cream, to which we could relate with some sense of security. Not so, very much less so at any rate, in the *Gaudete* epilogue and *Cave Birds*, in which the relation between the images and the known world is tenuous, and the poems show Hughes coining a new mythology in a new language in order to make himself at home in a world where order is lost and the literary heritage that nourishes the fantasy of it is irrelevant. Thus, rather than relate his vision to a familiar, concrete world and perform an act of organization on the chaos, he offers inconceivable images and jagged verse; and the catachreses come bucketing along, relating the unknown to the unimaginable.

Once again, nevertheless, Hughes comes back. After *Crow*, he returned to some exquisite description in *Season Songs*. After the dehumanized, rarefied work of the epilogue to *Gaudete* and of *Cave Birds*, he returns in the Moortown section of *Moortown* to the vivid presentation of animals, the sheep and cows, of his Devon farm, their births and deaths and the painful experiences in between. In *Crow* and in *Cave Birds*, Hughes dwells much on the mythological origins of his creatures—sometimes mechanical assemblages; in *Moortown*, he describes the kind of births known to biology, attended by all the muck and membranes of nature. They often go wrong: the poet must, for example, hack off the head of one half-born lamb in order to extract the rest of it. Occasionally, the urgent overwriting produces figures that obscure the object, but the poems generally provide the most vivid and accurate descriptions of animals that Hughes has ever produced. There is more of the sheer animalkind in them than in earlier poems, and there is much of the life of that awful farm of his where pain apparently prevails.

The pleasures of mimesis ("Ah, that is he") are not necessarily lost in the uncertainty of the poetry in these "brilliant extemporisations";[50] but for the vivid accuracy the poet has paid some artistic losses. A critic quotes a repetitious passage,

> I drive the battery
> As if I were hammering and hammering
> The frozen arrangement to pieces with a hammer
> And it jabbers laughing pain-crying mockingly
> Into happy life,

and exclaims, "Didn't he even read the thing over to pick up that 'Hammering . . . with a hammer'? If *Crow* was among other things an inferior parody of Blake, some of *Moortown* reads like an even worse parody of *that*."[51] The poems are certainly subject to various kinds of lapse. Another critic notes the "lack of concern with the artifices of making [that] displays a kind of arrogance which defeats criticism."[52] There is also a species of arrogance in some of the calculated ugliness and in the apparently gratuitous presentation of disgusting farm details. In the other parts of the volume, Hughes returns to the catachreses of *Cave Birds*, investing again in a practically private language for personal experiences virtually inaccessible to the reader. The volume offers a choice between our own palpable world in its proper sickening horror or the poet's private unrecognizable one, each in its own way repulsive.

In 1981, *Under the North Star* was published, with Hughes presenting wild animals again, rare northern ones but ones that do exist, in poems that are once more illustrated by Leonard Baskin. The paintings are superb, and in the poems there are a few details that show how well the poet sees. But the poems are, again, mythological. They dwell somewhat on birth, but the births have cosmic associations and lack the realism of the farm experience. The loon is "Hatched from the Moon"; in "The Muskellunge," the fish like

> An interplanetary torpedo
> Fell into the lake long ago
> When worlds were being made.

"Puma" presents a beast of the land, "the Cougar on the Mountain," ordained by God

> To be the organist
> Of the cathedral-shaped echoes.

Perhaps children, to whom the book is directed, find such figures more easily acceptable than do adults hardened by long commitment to common sense.

In such figures, as in most of the later poetry, Hughes is concerned with forces that are "out there," unfamiliar to most human experience. He is determined, at whatever heavy cost, to be strong and unafraid of the strong powers that have superseded civilization. His prevailing vision in the later poems is of a world in which violence is endemic and any human ordering a mere lingering vestige. It would be uncomfortable to believe that he is one of the unacknowledged legislators of the world.

As noted above, Hughes's career brings to mind at one point the descent into silence of some contemporaries. By the end of *Under the North Star*, he seems to have exhausted his various styles: the formal, traditional poetry has run into trivial rhymes; the concrete terms that convey the outrageous nonchalance of *Crow* have run into the footloose metaphors of *Cave Birds*; the profiles seen in early poems of the proud animals in nature have turned into the unedited presentations of the domestic beasts, their pathology, and their pain. The good poet of the early volumes has become programmed with the elements that, fresh and powerful in their original setting, are now a gray printout lacking the vitality and the sound of a human voice.

7

David Jones

David Jones, English in upbringing, was Welsh in his forebears and in his lifelong interest in the old traditions of Wales. His long poem *The Anathémata* concerns us in this book because, although published thirty years ago, it manifests one of the more remarkable departures in English poetic structure since *The Waste Land*. Its structure has been compared with that of the *Cantos* for the amassed detail, with that of *Ulysses* for the mythological substratum, and that of *Finnegans Wake* for the circularity. Unity has been seen in the progress of the Mass which, directly or obliquely, is repeatedly introduced, and in the poem's

---

David Jones (1895–1974) was of Welsh descent, and the traditions of his ancestors are carried on in his work. He attended art school and may be better known for his art than for his poetry. Jones worked for a while as an engraver, and he illustrated books for several years. From 1926 to 1956 he painted watercolors, mainly still life, landscape, and seascape; he held exhibitions in Venice, at the New York World's Fair, and at the Tate Gallery. But Jones was more than a simple graphic artist: he was among those who served on the Western Front in World War I, and he was among those who eloquently expressed the horror of that experience. So although Jones is included in this volume for the method with which he wrote, he belongs as well with the writers we most quickly associate with the First World War: Siegfried Sassoon, Wilfred Owen, Robert Graves, and others.

chronology.[1] Whatever structural principle may be claimed for it, however, the actual organization is deliberately loose. Jones was a painter and engraver and is known in literature chiefly for *The Anathémata* and *In Parenthesis*, the latter sometimes considered a novel. There are also *The Tribune's Visitation* and fragments of poems collected at the end of his life in *The Sleeping Lord*.

In Parenthesis, written between 1927 and 1929 and published in 1937, is partly in prose, partly in a loose verse, and partly—but only to a small extent—in rhyme. It is a presentation of the trench warfare in a sector of the western front from December 1915 to July 1916, telling with extraordinary vividness the experience of that singular time. The style is dominated by two major motives: first, to call forth the parallels in previous literature and myth by particular situations and incidents and to present them as if contemporary; and second, to reproduce the fierce realism of sensation. The realism is remarkable: from the tiny detail of a sensation all have experienced, a detail reproduced with a fidelity worthy of James Joyce—"Metalled eyelet hole in waterproof pall hanging glides cold across your upward tilted cheek"—to one that all can imagine—"The warm fluid [blood] percolates between his toes and his left boot fills, as when you tread in a puddle." And the images retain their power in longer descriptions, of which the following example is a part, showing at the end the sudden descent to a colloquial pitch that is a characteristic of both *In Parenthesis* and *The Anathémata*. Describing the new duckboards in the trench, Jones says, "Botched, ill-driven, half-bent-over nail heads protrude, where some transverse-piece jointed the lengthways, four-inch under-timber, marking where unskilled fatigue-man used his hammer awkwardly, marring the fairness of the thing made—also you trip up on the bleeder, very easily."[2] The response to bad craftsmanship as an affront is typical of

Jones, the craftsman, who registers elsewhere no sense of affront at all when a German throws a hand grenade in his direction. All the way through, the notes elaborate on allusions in the text to Welsh or Norse mythology, to details from Malory, the *Aeneid*, *The Golden Bough*, and the Bible. In his preface to *In Parenthesis*, Jones says of his time in the trenches, "At no time did one so much live with a consciousness of the past, the very remote, and the more immediate and trivial past, both superficially and more subtly."[3] One critic remarks of *In Parenthesis* and *The Tribune's Visitation* that Jones's warriors "seem to have a confusion of battles occurring simultaneously in their heads."[4] It has been claimed that the constant reference back constitutes the "mythical method" and identifies the war with previous ones.[5] Jones had read very little of Joyce but recognized within *In Parenthesis* "an oblique kind of" influence.[6]

The Anathémata, published in England in 1952 and in America in 1963, calls similarly upon the same ancient sources and others as well, especially Celtic. The subtitle is *Fragments of an Attempted Writing*. Jones thinks of the book as *anamnesis*, an act preserving things against oblivion; or perhaps it is rather an act of reclamation, to renew the validity of the old signs.[7] There are eight parts of unequal length, and their drifts—the endless series of variations, modulations, and embellishments on the Christian theme—are not always easy to follow. The first part, "Rite and Fore-Time," presents details of prehistory and the history of the foundation of Britain that in prefiguring and typology manifest the divine plan. "By the familiar Catholic argument," says Howard Nemerov, "that anything which is not Catholic is merely a natural prevision and inadequate vision of what is Catholic, even the geology of Great Britain is pictured as preparing itself for a sacred task as the matrix of the cultural form."[8] The prehistoric details are called deposits, the term being used also in its more literal geological sense. The poem begins with a description of the Mass, the sign, as Jones designates it, to which in one form or another the poem constantly returns. The Mass is associated with the voyage, as Jones explains in a later note: "What is pleaded in the Mass is precisely the argosy or voyage of the Redeemer, consisting of his entire sufferings and his death, his conquest of hades, his resurrection and his return in triumph to heaven. It is this that is offered to the Trinity . . . on behalf of us argonauts and of the whole argosy of mankind."[9] The poem is dominated, except in the last two parts, by nautical imagery: details of the Last Supper, for instance, are presented as follows:

> They set the thwart-boards
> and along:
> . . . .
> One for the swordsman [Peter], at the right-board,
> after;
> to make him feel afloat. . . .
> . . . .
> They make all shipshape
> for she must be trim
> . . . .
> Who d'you think is Master of her?[10]

But inasmuch as the Mass is to some degree a voyage, so the voyages in this work may in turn give a kind of presence to the Mass, even in parts of the poem with no Christian reference.

Part 2, "Middle-Sea and Lear-Sea," places the crucifixion in time with a number of references, including the following:

> Twelve hundred years
> close on
> since of the Seven grouped Shiners
> one doused her light[11]

—alluding to the extinction of one of the Pleiades when Troy fell. The poem then presents points of navigation of a ship sailing from the Mediterranean to Cornwall, carrying Roman explorers.[12] "Angle-Land," the third section, depicts the arrival of an Angle ship in British waters, the sea approaches, and the condition and the geography of part of England. There are no specific Christian references. In part 4, "Redriff," a carpenter addressing the representative of a Mediterranean sea captain, "the old Jason," refuses to hurry a repair job. Part 5, "The Lady of the Pool," the longest in the poem, is spoken by a cockney lavender seller, who is at times Augusta, identified with London. Her discourse is of London, anecdote, history, and legend of the city, the churches, the city port, and its shipping. Part 6, "Keel, Ram, Stauros," discusses the making of the keel, the battering ram, and the cross, exploiting the metaphorical potential of these wooden artifacts, all of which relate symbolically to the crucifixion, as in the following passage that echoes Gerard Manley Hopkins:

> Recumbent for us
> the dark of her bilges
> for fouled canopy
> the reek of her for an odour of sweetness.
> Sluiced with the seep of us
> knowing the dregs of us.
> Hidden wood
> tree that tabernacles
> the standing trees.
> Lignum for the life of us
> holy keel.[13]

Part 7, "Mabinog's Liturgy" (*Mabinog*, according to Jones's note, is "a tyro bard; and [*mabinogi*] meaning also a tale of infancy as in the tale called *Mabinogi Iesu Crist*")[14] presents the Incarnation, dating it as the crucifixion was dated in part 2, looking forward, in the manner of medieval lyrics,

from the birth to the crucifixion. The poet calls on legend-
ary figures to attend the Incarnation, comparing the beauty
of the Virgin with that of Venus, Helen, and Guinevere; he
also presents marvels associated with the first Christmas
and the duties of celebrants, including a description of the
fraternization on the western front, Christmas 1915. The
eighth part, "Sherthursdaye and Venus Day," Holy Thurs-
day and Friday, offers types and analogues of Christ, sacri-
ficial figures, the crucifixion, and finally the Mass.

The style is full of archaisms, hyphenated words, Welsh-,
Greek-, and Latinisms. The language is often harsh: Jones
cares for mellifluousness as little as Hopkins did. But he,
like Hopkins, is very concerned with the sound of his
poems. One fragment, "The Sleeping Lord," is, he says,
"essentially for the ear rather than the eye."[15] In all his
work, he assiduously supplies footnotes to describe pro-
nunciations, and allusions are often footnoted as well.
Jones ranges from Christian lore to Norse and Welsh folk-
lore; he finds analogues in Jewish history and legend,
in classical literature and myth, and in English literature
and popular song. Sometimes a note explains a private
association.

The Anathémata may proceed by massive phrases often
widely separated from what they qualify. In the first part,
"before" is repeated to introduce lengthy details of geological morphologies. Part 2, as the poem relates incidents
to the time of the crucifixion, includes long parallel passages: "Half a millennium or so / since . . ."; or "One hundred and sixty-seven years / since. . . ." In part 3, the word
"past" repeatedly introduces the names of places that the
ship sails by, their inhabitants, and anecdotes from their
histories. The carpenter of the fourth part emphatically
declines to hurry the job, with repeated hyperboles introduced with either "Not for" or "Not if." In part 5, "From"
introduces anecdotes of shipping that the Lady relates.

In many places the poem proceeds by questions: "What ages . . . ?" "How else . . . ?"

As in its substance the poem looks before and after for its analogues, so in its style one familiar recurring feature is the historic or prehistoric fact presented in the modern colloquial idiom or even embellished with an anachronistic detail from our own day. It is a ubiquitous feature: a vague allusion to a suspicious situation in 133 B.C. is concluded with

> the syndicate's agent
> pays-off the ranch operatives
> (his bit from the Urbs
> waits in the car).[16]

Underlying the tactic is the conception of art as anamnesis, recalling, and the poet's job as one of redeeming, "handing on such fragmented bits of our own inheritance as we have ourselves received."[17] The old signs must be made available, and "the poet, of whatever century, is concerned only with how he can use a current notion to express a permanent mythus."[18] The tactic is one that Pound used brilliantly in *Homage to Sextus Propertius*. Another example of it in *The Anathémata* illustrates as well a kind of personification made familiar in the later poems of W. H. Auden: "Just before they rigged the half-lit stage for dim-eyed Clio to step with small confidence the measures of her brief and lachrymal pavan."[19]

In such examples, David Jones is looking from the present world into the ancient, as in many watercolors he looks from the inside through a window to the world beyond: "I always work from the window of a house if it is at all possible. I like looking out on the world from a reasonably sheltered position."[20] Elsewhere he records the importance to the finished picture of the frame and mount, which can significantly add to or detract from the effect.[21]

135

Of the paintings containing windows, it is claimed that
"everything is fused into a vision where indoors and out-
doors, window and flowers and glass bowl and table lose
their identities and become, as it were, pure poetry." [22] This
may be so to some degree, as it is true to some degree that
spiritual things and material are both real. But the paintings, however visionary, are most often firmly anchored:
just as the down-to-earth modern phrases in *The Anathémata* catch the ear and eye of the reader, so in the paintings, among the uninsistent rhythms and reticulations in
the flowers and trees, there frequently appears an iron
window catch or a bit of the locking mechanism in hard
and stark outline, suggesting the kind of realism that contemporary colloquial language furnishes in the poetry. A
variant of this technique is at work in the passages of the
poetry in which terrible events are seen through the minds
of those for whom they are simply routine. It is a view-
point that Auden, once again, has used to advantage and
familiarized in such lines as these from "Terce," in the sequence "Horae Canonicae":

> After shaking paws with his dog,
> (Whose bark would tell the world that he is always kind,)
> The hangman sets off briskly over the heath.

Some of the fragments in Jones's work, "The Fatigue" particularly, dwell on the events of Passion Week from the
point of view of the soldiers garrisoned in Jerusalem, actors in the Passion for whom it meant "but one more guard,
fatigue or escort duty." [23]

The style rises to its highest pitch when Jones portrays
the crucifixion under terms of one or another elaborate
metaphor. From *The Anathémata*:

> tell the old Jason:
> As sure as I was articled, had I the job of mortisin'
> the beams to which was lashed and roved the Fault in all
> of

us, I'ld take m' time and set that aspen transom square to
the Rootless Tree.[24]

Jones notes elsewhere that for Fortunatus "the terrible
transom-beam of the instrument of our Manumission is
seen as a Roman steelyard exactly weighing the price."[25]
In "The Fatigue," there is a passage of natural history with
ominous undertones:

> the hill god
> who, from iron briars
> plucks flowers for all
> so clinking light they are
> to staple such a burdened bough
> on world-orchard wall.[26]

Finally in this series of passages figuring the crucifixion,
showing again the collision between contemporary language and practice and the historic event, is a passage,
which has been repeatedly and justly praised, that calls on
a number of poetic devices.

> It is the empty time
> after tiffin
> and before his first stiff peg.
> The fact-man, Europa's vicar
> The Samnite of the Pontian *gens*
> within the conditioned room
> sleeps on
> secure under the tiffany.
> They sting like death
> at afternoon.[27]

The constant reaching after parallels throughout the poem
makes for some depth of texture, but the richness of the last
quoted passage goes beyond what is typical in *The Anathémata*—the style is more typical with *In Parenthesis*, though
everywhere Jones is consistently alert to the connotations
and potential embroilments of words. "Peg" has its terrible
ulterior meaning; there is ironic play between "vicar" and

"Pontian"; "conditioned" is again ambiguous; and the use of death in a trivial, hackneyed hyperbole when the awful thing itself lurks in the offing with the added involvement of "sting" sets up powerful reverberations.

This kind of subtlety, going beyond the direct or oblique allusion to parallels, is unusual in *The Anathémata*, but it is consonant with principles of poetry Jones expressed in his preface to *The Anathémata*: "One of the efficient causes of which the effect called poetry is a dependant involves the employment of a particular language or languages, and involves that employment at an especially heightened tension. The means or agent is a veritable torcular, squeezing every drain of evocation from the word-forms of that language or languages. And that involves a bagful of mythus before you've said Jack Robinson."[28] The exploitation of the words, effective in the above passage from *The Anathémata*, calls, of course, for the cooperation of the reader. But what reader—even an archeologist or a Celtic scholar, or even one who has absorbed the glosses in the notes— what reader, it has been asked, can experience as poetry, the made thing, a passage such as the following—one that is not atypical.

> This he averred he achieved on his ocean-trip to the
>   Thing-
> Ness in Gynt-land, his *hiraeth* upon him, some fifteen days
> out from his *dinas* in Cemeis in Demetia
>   (where he latins his oghams).
> Plotting his course by the North Drift route that streams
> him warm to Hordaland
>   to Noroway o'er his faem
> over the gurly brim in his mere-hengest
>   (he's stepped the Yggdrasil for mast!)
> To the Horder's moot in Norvegia
>   over the darkening mere-flood
> on a Gwener-Frigdaeg noon.[29]

Because Jones is concerned with bringing together the current and the ancient, or elements that are separate by nature but susceptible of symbolic unity, his work makes much of typology. In *The Anathémata*, Hector is implicitly a type of Christ:

> When they regarded him:
> his beauties made squalid, his combed gilt
>   a matted mop
> his bruised feet thonged
>   under his own wall.
> Why did they regard him
> the decorous leader, *neque decor* . . .[30]

The Latin, "nor comeliness," is from Isaiah and used here to allude to Christ. There are more typological identities in "Keel, Ram, Stauros," as in the passage heavy with Hopkins. The typology includes, as we have seen, even the geology of Britain.

Although William Langland seems to have been the main conscious influence on his verse,[31] Jones has acknowledged admiration for Joyce and their affinity has been noted by T. S. Eliot, among others, in his introduction to *In Parenthesis*. Each has a "Celtic ear for the music of words," Eliot says, and both men's works call for "detective analysis," though Jones provides his with notes. Moreover, Jones, like Joyce, has been credited with the use of the "mythical method."[32] The method in question is that which Eliot attributed to *Ulysses*, in which events in the adventures of Odysseus are continually paralleled by the ordinary events of an ordinary day in the twentieth century in the life of Mr. Bloom. As Joyce alludes to myth to discover order, so, Monroe Spears argues, Jones refers everything to the Christian myth as an organizing principle. In all his work, he provides "a sense of dimension by relating contemporary subject matter to the mythical and historical archetypes and prototypes."[33] But although the Mass is in fact an organizing principle, there is still no representation of diurnal life to be thus organized as there is in *Ulysses*. The poem has no narrative like that of *In Parenthesis*. It is closer in this respect to *The Waste Land*, in which Eliot permits himself private associations, but *The Anathémata* is far more open to the vagaries of unschematic thoughts, "meanderings," as Jones calls them when he expresses his diffidence toward pattern and unity: "If it has a shape it is chiefly that it returns to its beginning. . . . If it has a unity it is that what goes before conditions what comes after and *vice versa*."[34] But the fragments that are mustered have come to mind "'in the time of the Mass.'" And "if pattern there is—these thought-trains (or, some might reasonably say, trains of distractions and inadvertence) have been as often as not initially set in motion, shunted or buffered into near sidings or off to far destinations, by some action or word, something seen or heard, during the liturgy."[35]

Despite his comments on unity and pattern, structure is important to Jones the artist: "Ars is concerned with the shape of a finished article."[36] *The Anathémata*, however, is fragments. But he is not committed to any simple meanings of "such words as 'finish,' 'form,' 'represent,' 'shape,' 'composition,'" and the like. In the practice of an art, "One learns something of the surprising contradictions and metamorphoses which such words must be made to cover if they are to be used other than in some narrow, arbitrary, convenient-for-the-occasion, academic or superficial sense."[37] Furthermore, the claims of the individual elements of the work over a regimenting structure are strong. In questioning a comment from Henry Reed, Jones says that "no 'external discipline' can be real, invigorating, and integrating unless it comes to us with the imperatives of a living tradition"; in 1953, the date of Jones's comment (originally in *The Listener*), he thought that no external discipline did.[38] He is, however, concerned with order and integration, unlike many modern and contemporary writers. External discipline might be associated with the withering power of the central government over the local scene: Jones is on the side of provinces, such as Wales. The theme of "The Fatigue," for example, is the ongoing collision between an imperial rule and an indigenous culture. The idea is of even greater importance in *The Tribune's Visitation*, in which the tribune, first haranguing his troops in the familiar manner of the superior officer, surprisingly speaks from the heart and confesses that empire calls for the death of regional culture:

> everything presuming difference
> and all the sweet remembered demarcations
>   wither
> to the touch of us
>   and know the fact of empire.[39]

The fragment is an engaging statement, and the tribune who speaks the whole thing is revealed in one or two clear strokes as a type of Christ.

Jones shows concern for the cost of organizing an empire or a poem; he would not be willing to organize at the risk of injuring the integrity of details. It has been said that he arranges the data of history "to make them point to the dignity of labour in the diverse service of man and God."[40] This may be so. But the order the poem possesses, of which we feel the pressure rather than the imposition, may be best conceived of by observing the analogous ordering principle in some of Jones's paintings. In the preface, Jones calls the fragments of *The Anathémata* "pieces of stuffs that happen to mean something to me. . . . Things to which I would give a related form, just as one does in painting a picture."[41] There are constant references to the

Mass, to memories of the particulars of the crucifixion and the cross, and there are the symbolic figures of the carpenter, the captain, the Lady, as well as the repeated figure of the ship—these, parts of the tradition, the mythus, create a kind of determination: details may be permitted to stray, having these points to which they constantly return. A quotation in Blamires suggests the structure is comparable to the design of a Celtic cross or manuscript: "What happens in a corner is as important as what happens at the centre, because there is often no centre."[42] The kind of relationship between organizing principle and detail that Jones seems to be creating in the poem is present, however, and may be literally seen in some of his watercolors, a comparison encouraged somewhat by Jones's own sense of the unity of his two artistic activities. Of one of his paintings he says, "There is a sense in which I regard this water-colour which I have just completed as belonging *imp*licitly to the same world of commemoration and anamnesis, as that to which *The Anathémata* belongs though here the apparent subject-matter is no more than some flowers in a glass *calix*."[43] What we observe in many of his watercolors is that in each an abundance of flowers, wayward and unaccountable, is strewn about one or more chalices or cups. The cups in their clear outline imply a limited sense of order, but their predominant feature is their transparence; the flowers, though they may radiate outward from the cup, are free. Lord Clark's comment on one of the later flower pieces is sensitive.

> The vase, broad and capacious like a Byzantine chalice of the eighth century, stands facing us on a plain table. Although no exclusively Christian symbol is visible, we at once have the feeling that this is an altar, and that the flowers in some way represent parts of the eucharist. There are wine-coloured carnations and ears of corn, thorny stems of roses and blood red petals, which drop onto the small white table-cloth. Yet none

of this is insisted on, and we are far from the closed world of symbolism. Every flower is there for a dozen reasons, visual, iconographical, or even on account of its name, and how far they can be interpreted as Christian imagery no one, perhaps not even the painter, can tell.[44]

The hint may be taken: we may consider the cup, which I suggest provides order, as the chalice or Grail and consider it thus as playing the same role as the Mass and the other Christian properties in *The Anathémata*, organizing fragments. The degree of order is limited, however, in both the paintings and the poem, for neither flowers nor fragments are trapped in "the closed world of symbolism."

There is a similar disposition of fragments and ordering principle in another painting: *Vexilla Regis* shows twined branches, a deer, horses, doves, brushed-up clouds; in the middle foreground there is the *vexillum*, the Roman standard, surmounted by the eagle; and all this is dominated in the foreground by the firm outlines of the tree and, wounding the tree, heavy dark nails. Again, Blamires has remarked, on the engraving "He Frees the Waters," how the elements of the dissolute, sinful world are grouped around the symbols of salvation, the lance and chalice. The pictures show the principle; their structure offers an analogy for the structure of *The Anathémata*—certain firmly presented vortices without compulsion attract other elements to gather about them. The "mythical method" is another thing.

8

Basil Bunting

Bunting is older than all the poets discussed in this book except David Jones; he belongs, however, with the experimental poets of this period. His early work goes back to the twenties, before Auden had established his strong magnetic pole; his major poem, *Briggflatts*, appeared in the sixties and is admired by all the younger writers who have attempted, as Bunting has, to break out of the tradition and to make poetry do what it has not habitually done.

Bunting was a friend and is a disciple of Pound, "one of Ezra's more savage disciples," according to W. B. Yeats. He visited Pound in Rapallo in 1929, arriving, it is reported, late at night and putting up at what he naively supposed to be a hotel, where he dreamed of women in dishabille visiting his bed. Pound explained in the morning. Pound,

---

Basil Bunting (b. 1900) is a graduate of the London School of Economics and has led a rather varied career. Aside from being a poet, Bunting has served as an editor with several journals, including *Transatlantic Review, Paris, Music Critic, The Outlook,* and *London.* Moreover, Bunting spent some time working for *The Times* of London as its Persian correspondent. He has held the presidency of both the Poetry Society (1972–1976) and Northern Arts (1973–1976). The University of Newcastle upon Tyne has honored Bunting not only with an honorary Doctor of Letters degree but also by granting the status of Honorary Life Visiting Professor.

Basil Bunting

"village explainer," as Gertrude Stein called him, must also have explained a lot of literary things to Bunting: the work of no other English poet, except perhaps Ronald Bottrall, is as close to Pound's as his; the admiration of no one else is as great. Bunting learned from Malherbe, Dante, and Persian poets, and from Chaucer, Wyatt, Spenser, and other English masters. But Pound is preeminent in his regard, having done for the twentieth century, he claims, what Spenser did for the Elizabethans. He has followed Pound, for some random examples, in the poem of factual detail (here the cage label in the zoo) followed by the throw-away ending:

> ♂ Felis Tigris (Straits Settlements) (Bobo) takes exercise
> up and down his cage before feeding
> in a stench of excrements of great cats
> indifferent to beauty or brutality.
> He is said to have eaten several persons
> but of course you can never be quite sure of these things.[1]

He has followed "Hugh Selwyn Mauberley" in the sentiment, the tone, and the form of the following:

> Each sour noon
> squeezed into teashops
> displays one at least
> delicate ignorant face
>
> untroubled by
> earth's spinning
> preoccupied rather
> by the set of her stocking.[2]

He has obviously admired Pound's jewelry and Canto XLV.

> See! Their verses are laid
> as mosaic gold to gold
> gold to lapis lazuli
> white marble to porphyry

145

> stone shouldering stone, the dice
> polished alike, there is
> no cement seen and no gap
> between stones as the frieze strides
> to the impending apse.[3]

Throughout the early work there is much of Pound. And *Briggflatts* is surely the most exquisite product in twentieth-century poetry of the use of Pound—the method, somewhat, and the voice—in a poem that in many other respects, its traditional allegiance, its setting, vocabulary, and sounds, is more exclusively English than anything else in the century. It is the poetry of a man returned from a long sojourn abroad, proud of his Northumbrian heritage: "The Northumbrian tongue travel has not taken from me."[4]

In all Bunting's work, however, in addition to what he derived from Pound, there is a musical element. Pound describes his own poetry as "painting or sculpture just coming over into speech," and the description fits much of his verse, as it fits also much of Bunting's. But in *Briggflatts* there is this:

> Flexible, unrepetitive line
> to sing, not paint; sing, sing,
> laying the tune on the air.

And throughout Bunting's work there is music: first, purely and simply, in the tones and rhythms of vowels and consonants audible, especially among monosyllables,[5] such a music as is not to be readily detected in Pound. Both early and late in Bunting's career, this music is remarkable, from a 1928 description of London in the rain, "Pools on the bustop's buttoned tarpaulin,"[6] to

> Brag, sweet tenor bull,
> descant on Rawthey's madrigal,

each pebble its part
for the fells' late spring,

the opening lines of *Briggflatts*. Or there is this from the same poem:

Even a bangle of birds
to bind sleeve to wrist
as west wind waves to east
a just perceptible greeting—
sinews ripple the weave,
threads flex, slew, hues meeting,
parting in whey-blue haze.

A hundred examples of this kind of music might be adduced from the *Collected Poems*: nowhere are the canons of free verse so eminently justified. The tones are more consistently effective than those consistently achieved by Ezra Pound. Bunting acknowledges also the influence of Louis Zukofsky, who uses not only melodic tones and cadences in his work but also musical structures.

In *Briggflatts*, there are musical considerations other than the effects of collisions between consonants and vowels. There are, for example, images that reappear throughout and provide motifs after the fashion of music: the bull, the phallic slowworm, the mason and his craft, the spider web, and the names of musical instruments. Indeed, it is claimed that *Briggflatts* has a symphonic structure: "fragments of themes are presented in the first four movements gradually, taking on more significance each time a fragment relating to the same block of thematic material is repeated, until in the fifth and final movement, the fragments are brought together in a resolution which combines all the basic subject matter of the poem, art and experience, love and memory, nature and the cosmos."[7] This may be oversimplification, but there is no doubt that Bunting had musical considerations in mind while making the poem. Bunting has described composition as beginning with a form vaguely in the mind that is an irritation until it can be got down on the page. He begins with shapes of sounds: he can see the whole shape before he begins the difficult task of filling out the parts. The poem only exists as sound.

Charles Tomlinson finds that Bunting's art aspires to a condition of music and that the achievement of *Briggflatts* "derives from the attempt to bring Then into as close a relation with Now as possible. The aligning of the two comes about by the central device of imitating 'the condition of music.' Then and Now are brought upon each other as are the different voices in a madrigal."[8] It is best, perhaps, to be judiciously vague about the musical analogy; a good anthology safely attributes to the poem an attempt at "something like a musical form."[9] The general musical effect, however, is so manifest that it sometimes seems proper in describing the evolution of the poet's mood in the poem to say of this or that passage not that it describes or presents but that it *is*—the height or depth or whatever.

One line in the poem reads, "Follow the clue patiently and you will understand nothing"; Bunting has declared, "History points to an origin that poetry and music share, in the dance that seems to be a part of the make up of *homo sapiens*, and needs no more justification or conscious control than breathing."[10] Of *Briggflatts*, he says it is beauty and not meaning he is after, a comment that, considering that the poem is a structure of words, seems a bit self-defeating.[11] "Or if you insist on misusing words," his comment goes on, "its 'meaning' is of another kind, and lies in the relation to one another of lines and patterns of sound . . . which the hearer feels rather than understands."[12] In another medium, Alain Robbe-Grillet similarly bids the audience experience *Last Year at Marienbad* as addressed exclusively to its sensibilities—sight, hearing, and feeling.[13] The mind of the ordinary reader, however, is not disciplined to hear only sounds and ignore meaning any more than it is easily able to perceive the colors of an object as mere colors without their structural relationships—the exercise discussed by Whitehead and noted above.

In *Briggflatts*, however, structural lines are detectable in the content, shadowy though they may be. There are the two time periods Tomlinson mentions: the identification of these, when Then becomes Now, brings together that of the poet as youth and that of the man with sixty or more winters on his head; beyond both times is the day of Eric Bloodaxe, who for two years in the tenth century was king of Northumbria. Then, again faint enough, there is the outline of a progression from youth, through a quest, an inferno, and degradation, to return and renewal. The first part of the poem contains its most firm and vivid images, presenting sights and sounds of the good English rural life, the bull, may (hawthorn), a fire of oak and applewood,

> sour rye porridge from the hob
> with cream and black tea,
> meat, crust and crumb,

rain, the slowworm, and others; Chaucer himself was not more English. A stonemason is lettering a gravestone; a young couple travel across North England in the mason's cart, lying on the stone, sheltered by sacks from the rain. They make love before a kitchen fire. In this section of the poem, young love and death are juxtaposed; there is also a motif that reappears later of life emerging from death and decay:

> Decay thrusts the blade,
> wheat stands in excrement
> trembling.

The following lines, however, present the most important theme of the poem:

> The mason stirs:
> Words!
> Pens are too light.
> Take a chisel to write.

In the last section of part 1, there is a sudden change of pitch:

> Dung will not soil the slowworm's
> mosaic. Breathless lark
> drops to nest in sodden trash.

This change may suggest a sonata form like that of Scarlatti, whom Bunting praises later in the poem.

Part 2 opens with a description of the poet's role and reminds us that *Briggflatts* is subtitled "An Autobiography," Bunting having observed, however, that it is the spiritual autobiography of any artist.[14] The poet is despised and degraded; he is a recording eye, like Mauberley, but less fussy.

>   he gauges
> lines of a Flemish horse
> hauling beer, the angle, obtuse,
> a slut's blouse draws on her chest.

But he fulfills his duty in squalor; like Pound's Odysseus,

> He lies with one to long for another,
> sick, self-maimed, self-hating,
> obstinate, mating
> beauty with squalor to beget lines still-born.

Next, the poet is the pilot of a ship of which the crew "grunt and gasp" and see nothing that he sees. His art is ignored;

> Who cares to remember a name cut in ice
> or be remembered?
> Wind writes in foam on the sea.

And what the sea writes merely reinforces the theme of forgetfulness.

Shortly, the mason's materials are introduced: the marble split from the Apuan Alps, the chisel from iron ore, smelted, ground, and sharpened. But the mason, like the poet later, betrays his craft:

> a reproached
> uneasy mason
>
> shaping evasive
> ornament
> litters his yard
> with flawed fragments.

There follows a description of the death of Bloodaxe and a hint of his moral failure "loaded with mail of linked lies." Finally, redeeming the conception of the craftsman's trade, an image of Pasiphae receiving the bull, the god, and the spirit glorying in "unlike creation."

Part 3 presents a Dantean (and Poundian) hell of coprophagists, hags, hovels, corpses, disease, and other horrors. The poet is identified here with Alexander,[15] who alone, among companions desiring their home, strikes out for the mountain peak and gains a vision of Israfel, the colossal Muslim archangel who will blow the trumpet for the day of judgment. Then to the poet's ear comes the chanting of a song by the slowworm as it celebrates its oneness with the natural world, restoring the poet, who "rose and led home silently through clear woodland."

In the fourth part, an heroic past, when Aneurin the Welsh bard immortalized battle, has ebbed like floodwater. Poetry that had been splendor reflecting splendor has now decayed into a "pedant's game"; the ear has become too gross for the old good kind:

> Can you trace shuttles thrown
> like drops from a fountain, spray, mist of spiderlines
> bearing the rainbow, quoits round the draped moon;

> shuttles like random dust desert whirlwinds hoy at their
>   tormenting sun?
> Follow the clue patiently and you will understand nothing.

From contemplating the decay of his art, however, the poet rallies to praise Scarlatti. Then he presents images of his love:

> My love is young but wise. Oak, applewood,
> her fire is banked with ashes till day.
> The fells reek of her hearth's scent,
> her girdle is greased with lard;
> hunger is stayed on her settle, lust in her bed.
> . . . .
> Her scones are greased with fat of fried bacon,
> her blanket comforts my belly like the south.

These lines reflect the earlier passage that describes the young couple sharing farmhouse food and physical love. Here, though, the experience is ripened and jaded with time. An English critic speaks of "most appetising country comforts" in connection with these lines. He must know what kindles his appetite, but the connotations convey a hardening of the earlier situation: "ashes," "reek," "grease," "lust," "belly." The poet is degraded, no longer Alexander. But he is still defiant:

> Where rats go go I,
> accustomed to penury,
> filth, disgust and fury;
> . . . .
> O valiant when hunters
> with stick and terrier bar escape
> or wavy ferret leaps.

Part 5 is the resurgence of the poet's spirit, declaring the winter solstice gone and the "years end crescendo." In this mood, the poet finds order and beauty in decay and squalor: maggots

group a nosegay
jostling on cast flesh,
frisk and compose decay
to side shot with flame,
unresting bluebottle wing. Sing,
strewing the notes on the air.

"Silver blades of surf" shape "the shore as a mason . . . his stone." There follow images of sheep, shepherds, and the sheepdogs of the Northumberland dales. Then this:

the river praises itself,
silence by silence sits
and Then is diffused in Now.

The fifty years between the youths of the first part and the aging poet and his aging beloved are elided; in this shaped harmony, Then is Now: "Capella floats from the north / with shields hung on his gunwale." The shields on the gunwale recall Bloodaxe who came from Norway, supposedly, in a boat thus appointed. The light from Capella,

light from the zenith
spun when the slowworm lay in her lap
fifty years ago,

actually "set out 45 years ago," a note tells us, but Bunting adds that that span is "as near fifty as makes no difference to a poet."[16] The images carry us back again to part 1: the young, physical sexuality of that day is identified now with love and night.

Starlight quivers. I had day enough.
For love uninterrupted night.

The poem seeks no neat ending by recapitulation and conclusion, however, ending with a coda, in a rhythm that has been described as being the rhythm of the sea.[17] And the substance is not a grateful completion of the previous material but an outward questioning.

Where we are who knows
of kings who sup
while day fails? Who,
swinging his axe
to fell kings, guesses
where we go?

Bunting has nudged *Briggflatts* away from the direct course of argument or narrative toward the condition of music, and elements of musical structure, as we have seen, are manifest. Yet neither the general aspiration to be like music, an aspiration quite common in this age, nor the shadowy structure of the quest accounts entirely for the nature of the poem, which we may envisage by focusing on the concept of "unlike creation," the achievement of Pasiphae with the bull (and the achievement of the singing bull in the opening lines). Such a creation is this auto-biographical poem itself, the rendering of a life in words. In this respect, of course, the poem is no different from any other autobiographical poem. The poet of *Briggflatts*, though, is conscious of his poetic activity within the poem itself. Words are in part units of melody and musical struc-ture as well as units of meaning; the musical use is, again, an instance of unlike creation. The poem repeatedly takes its substance from music, as well as deriving shape from it. In the fourth part, for an example, Bunting says,

It is time to consider now Domenico Scarlatti
condensed so much music into so few bars
with never a crabbed turn or congested cadence,
never a boast or a see-here; and stars and lakes
echo him and the copse drums out his measure,
snow peaks are lifted up in moonlight and twilight
and the sun rises on an acknowledged land.

"Acknowledged" suggests that here, as in other literature from Plato to Wallace Stevens, music orders experience. The identifying of Scarlatti's cadence with landscape, how-ever, points again to the matter of unlike creation. Earlier, in part 2, the poem identifies objects in nature with pieces of music:

> Starfish, poinsettia on a half-tide crag,
> a galliard by Byrd.
> . . . .
> Asian vultures riding on a spiral
> column of dust
> or swift desert ass startled by the
> camels' dogged saunter
> figures sudden flight of the descant
> on a madrigal by Monteverdi.

The musical identity here again symbolizes order: "Anemones spite cullers of ornament / but design the pool," the poem continues, "But who will entune a bogged orchard, / its blossom gone."

Part 2 contains also a series of passages in which the poet, a deserter from direct verbal expressions, renders the poem itself as a series of items perceived with all the senses in turn:

> It tastes good, garlic and salt in it,
> with the half-sweet white wine of Orvieto
> . . . .
> It sounds right, spoken on the ridge
> between marine olives and hillside
> . . . .
> It feels soft, weed thick in the cave
> and the smooth wet riddance of Antonietta's
> bathing suit . . .
> . . . .
> It looks well on the page, but never
> well enough. Something is lost
> when wind, sun, sea upbraid
> justly an unconvinced deserter.

In frustration over his imperfect ability to express himself in words, the poet constantly holds words in counterpoint to other modes of expression, other unlike creations such as the chiseled stone. The artist must be cautious in choosing a medium, however; for example,

> Name and date
> split in soft slate
> a few months obliterate.

Then there are the images of the wind shaping the sea, and the surf and shore, another alternative species of creation.

In *Briggflatts*, Bunting has deliberately suppressed meaning. A musical structure need not do so; *Four Quartets* and *The Ghost Sonata*, formed according to music, are not so opaque. We are to understand that a direct meaning betrays the experience, an acceptance now commonplace in poetic theory. Thus, out of concern not to betray the real, Bunting deserts his craft. Because the pen is "too light," the poet needs a chisel (though later the mason's craft is also infirm). For his autobiography, therefore, the poet offers the unlike creation of a dance of images that are to appeal to various unlike senses. But the dance *is still in the making*; *Briggflatts*, like *Paterson*, reveals the poet's understanding that the poem is still in process, a process honored by Bunting. If *Briggflatts* can be said to have a subject, it is the act of making a poem. In "At Briggflatts Meeting House," the last poem of the sequence titled "The Second Book of Odes," Bunting elaborates this theme. The poem begins in the blunt and obscure style of Robert Browning:

> Boasts time mocks cumber Rome. Wren
> set up his own monument.

Then the heavily stressed syllables associated with Rome, Wren, and permanence are replaced by an uninsistent liquid rhythm.

> Yet for a little longer here
> stone and oak shelter
>
> silence.

Opposed to those claiming permanence, "we" ask "nothing but silence." And in return we are granted the final image:

> Look how clouds dance
> under the wind's wing, and leaves
> delight in transience.

Life inheres in not arriving at permanence; on the same principle, a firm structure is avoided.

9

Anselm Hollo

For Anselm Hollo, William Carlos Williams made writing possible; Hollo has declared that among his sources is Williams's "awareness of all animate and inanimate objects (and subjects) around him." The animate and inanimate objects of which Hollo is aware are not, for the most part, selected for their conventional significance; and, presented in varied rhythms in free verse, they lack whatever point and emphasis might have been derived from a regular verse form. That such things as he presents should be presented as they are—indeed that they should be presented at all—suggests that to Hollo as to many of his contemporaries there is importance in the usual activities of men and women and in the ordinary objects with which they

Anselm Hollo (b. 1934, as Paul Anselm Alexis) could be considered Finnish, British, or American. Although his background is Baltic-Finnish, he spent many years working and writing in Britain before moving to the United States. After working for the BBC in London (1958–1966), Hollo has become part of the American mainstream of poets—that is, he writes and teaches in universities, in writing programs that help to promote poetry in this country by providing an atmosphere in which young men and women can share their art and ideas. Aside from his participation in programs at Bowling Green (Ohio) State University, Hobart and William Smith Colleges, and SUNY Buffalo, Hollo has taught at the University of Iowa and most recently at New College of California in San Francisco. A past co-editor of *The Iowa Review*, he was also head of the Translation Workshop there in 1971–1972.

have commerce. He is absorbed by the fairness of the passing moment and is self-conscious in his absorption and pleasure in the observation of it—and he bids it stay:

> two young girls
> with long, red-golden hair
> over identical short fur coats (black)
>   walking, fast
> to some pleasurable place.
>
> I enjoy saying it
>   so slowly.[1]

The moment can offer its seemingly simple pleasures to the ear,

> most of the time we sit down
> to write 'sitting down' down,[2]

or to the eye,

> A Volkswagen bus
> full of greens.[3]

There is a good deal of play in Hollo, especially in the later volumes: *Maya*, the title of his 1970 collection, bears as epigraph the following lines, which are attributed to "Robin Williamson (The Incredible String Band)":

> Maya
>
>   Maya
>
> all this world is but a play
>   be thou   the joyful player

We may regard these poems as invitations to participate in the environment and become one with it, for no one more than Hollo calls us more clearly to the things of this world.

His act of entering into such relationship with the world, however, is sometimes accompanied in the poems by that strange experience in which part of the mind leaves the body, and the poet becomes the object, as well as the agent,

159

of observation, an object or thing of this world. The migrating part might be called the astral body: in *Alembic*, Master Rudolph is quoted as saying, *"Man today is composed of a Physical Body, of an Ethereal Body, of an Astral Body, and of an Ego."*[4] The poet may speak of "he who was I," say "he was me," or describe the setting of "A House A Street A Night":

> I am outside & inside, I stand
> in front of that house
>   in front of this house
>   a dark house . . .
> I look at it & know that I'm inside.[5]

In *Maya*, the poet's participation involves a similar dissociation:

> I'm not here, in this poem
> I'm in another room, writing praises
>   of their loveliness & terror
> the long-haired beings that dance through my mind.[6]

Two of the curious graphic designs in the volume *& it is a song* may be associated with the participation motif, the second one negatively. One, a cubical arrangement of slabs, surmounted by two heads, one inverted and the other broken, bears the words "dirges," "laments," "homages," and the names "J. F. K.," "Apollinaire," "Pythagoras," "Henry Miller," "Patrice Lumumba," "Artaud," and others. In the forefront is the word "HEADS" in block capitals and, centrally placed, the large but lowercase letter "i." In the section of the volume that follows, the poems present some of the people named as having been active and lively but now destroyed. The poet, who appears in his works quite frequently as "i," admires activity, and fears death, is perhaps identifying himself with these figures. In the second design, the word "ego-centric," the opposite of participation, is surrounded by names of plants, animals, and things—including red pianos, endless staircases, meditations—that, again, appear in the poems following.

A graphic design in the center of the volume shows three ornately stylized candles, increasing slightly in size, the tallest to the right. Below them is the word "TROBAR"; above are three lines of its etymology and cognates, including "*trouver* find f. LL *tropare* makes poetry." The design is related to the poem on the page facing it, "Trobar: To Find," which gives a clue to one feature of Hollo's method—discovery by way of metaphor. First, the poet sees the moon in the window, but it is not his window. Second, he questions what he has seen. Third, he makes a trope:

"The moon—

in the window?" yes

ma domna

—this last phrase is the Provençal, hence troubadour, word for *my lady*. The third part concludes by integrating parts by means of the figure of speech.

can it be
can it be ma domna! I'm singing
& it is a song

The third part (equivalent, maybe, to the third and tallest candle) suggests that the trope has banished the uncertainty of the experience of seeing the moon and has made it a song. And perhaps, although Hollo's poems do not regularly encourage a backward glance to their beginnings, the poet has made the experience a possession by making it a song.

Many of the poet's perceptions are of things as seen through the eyes of a child or they are, more generally, childlike. Hollo sees an eighteen-month-old stumping up a hill and recognizes she is

161

> seeing only the ground
>   move away
> under her feet.[7]

The poet's own child with its perceptions is often present in a poem; and we recall the anecdote about Paul Klee who, when challenged that his paintings could have been done as well by a child, agreed and included his own child Felix. In one poem, the child sits

> On a grey carpet, in a yellow sacklike garment
> Gently rocking to Dixieland jazz
> And contemplating a sliver of tinfoil
>   its ever-changing shape.[8]

Or the young Tamsin plays word games:

>   *
>
> orange schubert
>   *
>
>   this
>   my car
> big battered shoe.[9]

Many of the adult perceptions in these poems have child-like appearances because they are recorded without an organizing context. A number of poems are brief, sometimes consisting of a single perception only. Longer poems are frequently spaced across the page, words are separated by blanks, preserving thus a kind of isolation. It might be claimed for them as for isolated phrases in Ezra Pound that, on account of the silences that separate them, they are sharper and more exciting than if they were closely set in a verbal context.

On the other hand, Hollo says that the pleasure of a poem like Williams's "Red Wheelbarrow" is not in the precision of the observation or the "thingness" so much as in the dreamlike quality of it, "like an early childhood memory."[10] He speaks in a poem of "walking & talking dreams" that compose "the continuous & projective field."[11] A number of poems record what are apparently actual dreams, including the poem "bits of soft anxiety," for example:

dreamt: crossroads
drove straight ahead
arrived then with some confusion beating of wings sound
  of great engines et cetera.[12]

Another poem, whose title is its first words, begins,

Where was it? I

fell asleep in the afternoon
    & down & into a hall
        where forceful as ever in her big chair
he who was i there saw her.[13]

Some of the poet's dreams are "black crowded" and contain a nightmare projection of the self:

the horses' heads bobbing up & down within
his own   their wooden lips drawn back
from rotting wooden teeth   meaning him

meaning him & what would become of him.[14]

The dreaminess is at times replaced by the surreal, but more often there is amusement at the surrealist character or the amusing incongruities of everyday reality. "The Fiends" describes police searching for marijuana in a baby carriage.

        2 babies on top
    surprised at bobbies
    groping around their damp bottoms.[15]

In "Evensong," also from *Faces and Forms*, a military scientist happily listens to Ray Charles on his hi-fi, thinking it is Maria Callas, his ears clogged with radioactive dust. A poet singing in the fields sees

a cow stop grazing to listen

he was enchanted

but when he looked closer
realized she was simply peeing.[16]

The observation of quotidian detail is often a source
of amusement, one way or another, but throughout the
poems there is among these trivia a recurring concern
with forward movement. Poems, Hollo declares in the
words of Philip Whalen, are "graphs of a mind moving."[17]
Despite Hollo's occasional ambivalence toward going forward, his poems, like those of many of his contemporaries, tend to move on, from one thing to another. They
do so in the fashion prescribed by Charles Olson's "Projective Verse" essay and parallel to the post-Newtonian
concept of reality, in a developing process that forms new
patterns as it moves. Some of Hollo's later poems proceed
without a backward glance; "out of this world," for example, lists events and at no point turns back on itself, concluding with this passage.

        dark blur girl
    rushing
            past in a car

    a lifetime.
    where was she going
    *

    hi—
    late summer.
                all
                    is forgiven
    *

    ovidius naso
    wrote a book

    sir vincent wigglesworth
    created a giant caterpillar

    here
        I put them together

    (you do too)
    *

thales of miletus
loved
    this humid universe
there are
such advantages
    to walking on 2 legs
    & carrying
        one's brain in one's head
let the galaxies
      ride!
        thales
  it's been a long time
      between drinks.[18]

Between, that is, the water from which the earth originated, according to Thales, and the water to which he believed it would return. The poem moves steadily forward, with unlike items such as Ovid and Wigglesworth forced violently into juxtaposition; yet if the silences between the heterogeneous items be observed, it is possible that they not only will supply the kind of sharpening noticed above but also will serve as a substitute for an organizing principle. Hollo thus permits the mind to receive and lodge the items separately without the shock it undergoes with packed sequences of surreal images. It is possible. And this may be what the closing comments of an earlier poem, "the day's events," are intended to convey about the order of sentences:

not knowing the right order,
  how could i deny it.
it is there, with the silence,
  between the sentences.[19]

Such is not always Hollo's manner. In certain earlier poems the reader is not free to consider elements separately, though their relationship may be quite illogical. The title poem of *The Man in the Treetop Hat* supplies a wild variety of images that look back and are entangled with each other.

> hundreds of yellow
>   leaves
>   swirling around her feet
> his cries were lost in the wind inside
> his head
>   & she looked puzzled, puzzled
>   & beautiful.
> They kept on coming
>   a frieze,
> carrying breasts & tall jars
> O smiles of centuries.

Some poems emphasize their own rapid forward movement; "bang bang with a silencer" begins,

> watching the screens
> all that dying
>   the mind goes faster
>   won't stop to wait for words,[20]

and then, following a short procession of details, the poem closes,

> walk faster comrades
> into the time that will be.

In other poems, however, the forward movement is countered by images of enclosure:

> frightened
>   they close the glass case
>   over themselves & their lovers.[21]

In "La Noche,"

> the city is a great dragon   it is a procession
>   it is on the move
> but the curtains are drawn.[22]

Indeed, curtains seem to inhibit life:

> three years we have lived here
> with no curtains to hide us
>
> moving more freely
> summer nights.[23]

The ambivalence toward forward movement is seen in the symbolic adventurer Odysseus, who appears in several of Hollo's poems. The poem "Instances" refers to Zeus's command that Calypso let Odysseus go—a movement that would be at once forward from Ogygia yet back to Ithaca.

> nice place ya got here
> the Messenger said
> to her whose island
> it was
> > but the boss
> give an order:
> let the guy sail
> back to his own.[24]

In its version in Maya (1970), the poem concludes with ambivalence affirmed, as Odysseus asks, "Who said I wanted to go?" In "the going-on poem," which does not by any means move relentlessly forward but repeats images and ideas and recoils back into memory, the hero is countered by Winnie the Pooh, the famous teddy bear of A. A. Milne's children's books. The poem consists of impulses from the poet's environment, the backyards of the London suburb of Fulham, and his meditations upon them. The trees in the backyards, he tells a small boy, are not junipers such as scented the cloak given to Odysseus. The boy's voice blends with the notes of the pigeons, and the poet meditates upon communities. Shortly, upon hearing the church bell, he reflects on the community of Christians in Fulham. Then there is another external impulse:

> a shooting occurred
> between the last two lines.
> > *james meredith!*
> the man shouted
> > *james meredith!*
> & shot him
> in the back.[25]

Toward the end of the poem, this shooting is related to that performed by Odysseus in the great hall.

The poem proceeds by external stimuli, meditations, and associations, even suggesting of itself, "slowly it goes, but it goes / and if it doesn't go, we make it go." The poem is open to any direction that stimuli or association may turn it, as Allen Ginsberg's "Wichita Vortex Sutra," in which, as he drives, the poet sees road signs and hears bits from the radio and meditates upon them. But Ginsberg's poem has a center, the violence of Carrie Nation that rippled outward to become the violence of the Vietnam War; "the going-on poem" has none. In addition to responding to external events, however, the poet calls upon memory and comes up with Winnie the Pooh:

> > juniper,
> smell of memory.
> > to give in
> to one's mind.
> > winnie the pooh
> going upstairs,
> > bump, bumpety, bump.

As the counterpart of Odysseus, Pooh is soft, while the other—in the context of the shooting in the great hall—is cruel. The poet is identified with both:

> you grow up a lonely child
> & want to become a hero,
> soft & cruel.

Odysseus represents the traveler, going on, but he shares

the stage with the bear who, here and in other poems by Hollo, is warm, soft, happy, and, above all, stationary and secure.

Recourse to childhood security and beyond it to prenatal existence is frequent in this poet. Repeatedly in the early poems, when he would or should be an Odysseus with the mind on the move, he is drawn into the lair of the soft animal, where he is secure and may dream, like a child in its mother's arms or a fetus in the womb. Such retreat is often accompanied by a humming sound.

The withdrawal takes various forms. In a short poem, "The Alarm," for one tiny instance, the horn from a neighbor's MG sticks, and

> round-eyed
> cradling each other
> we waited
> waited.[26]

The place of security may be a small dark room, or a dark house. It may be the inside of a mountain, as in "Three bear poems," where the poet is

> looking for a bear   to take me to the mountain
> the glorious city inside the mountain
> where all the lost people go.[27]

Or the secure place may be that in which new life originates, as in "spring fever bear post-hibernation songs," in which newness emerges from the "dream-hole":

> it was hot in the dream-hole
> there was light in the dream-hole
> there was smoke in the dream-hole
> music & dark & staggering dreams.[28]

In another poem, lovers shed their clothes and discover

> standing
> naked
> between us a sudden clearing in space
> humming as if to give birth to a sun.[29]

Or in their dream the lovers are Adam and Eve, "the first two moles / in earth," making love "in the humming darkness," giving birth to ecstasies and visions. The place where new life is awaited may even be a mailbox, from which the poet is ready to clamber out

> when the horn
> is sounded by airmail angels
> travelling on a pale green wind
> we lie listening for,
> having had word.[30]

Or it may be a plane, as in "To be born again"; after being born from his mother, the poet enters "another plane,"

> walk right into it
>
> the roaring begins
> a few hours later
> i stride ashore
> "welcome to america."[31]

There is a humming sound again in another poem, in which a vast image of a beast appears to symbolize, as in Yeats, the birth of a new order:

> not far from here, in a shadow
>   or cluster of shadows
>   not my own
> a large beast is turning, half-waking
> moving a heavy head slowly
> a hum as of generators in pain or of pain around it.[32]

There are poems, then, in which the poet moves actively ahead, and there are others in which he has retreated into a dark enclosure or into the shadows, where new life of a kind may be awaited or generated, although both action and withdrawal may come in a single poem. The one from which the image of the beast is drawn, "the day's events," shows how Hollo faces some of the problems of writing a poem and demonstrates something of his methods and concerns. It begins in swift movement: two girls walking fast (the lines are quoted above), a sparrow buzzing a cat. Then comes a brief meditation, "World War Three / going on all the time," followed by "an old mumble   on a park bench" and more activity, with the eighteen-month-old child "stumping up the hill" and trying to catch the dog. Then, the poet returns to reflection:

> there is pain,
>   who can deny it.
> there is joy,
>   who can deny it.
> the ultra-intelligent machine
>   is what we need.

The machine is presumably a presiding genius that would organize, order, and bring meaning to the shifting ratios of pain and joy. Our need of it is like our need for a mother, in whose absence, in the passage that follows, the "toys in the nursery   fail in their power." The female figure here is archetypal:

> She wants us to love her
>   in all her daughters
> She is her own mothers
> She is all her daughters.

In response to problems he sees in the relationship, Hollo suggests,

> what we need to do is write
> a lot of sentences
> & then put them in the right order
> if we know the right order.

The remark about World War III is repeated. If we knew the right order, presumably the day's events and the background of the Vietnam War could be integrated in a conventional poem.

The question of the right order comes up implicitly elsewhere in Hollo. In "Blue Dream Movie in Eleven Takes,"[33] for example, the lines are numbered but out of order. Following the reference to the war in "the day's events" is the image of the beast, after which is an allusion to a poet, presumably Ted Hughes, and to the loss of "she whom he loved," for whom the present poet is reading praise from the Book of the Dead. Concluding the poem come images of both closure and movement, as well as the passage quoted above about silence:

> closing the book,
>   switching off the light.
>
> going from this room
>   to her, to you.
>
> not knowing the right order.

The poem is uncharacteristic of much of Hollo's work inasmuch as it turns back on itself with repetitions and is dominated by two strong images, the archetypal female, "she," and the half-waking beast, which have a depth generally alien to his work. Characteristically, on the other hand, it is an open poem into which, as into "the going-on poem," miscellaneous perceptions are free to enter. It offers none of the satisfactions derived from conventional form but instead the interest of perceptions vivid in their respective isolations.

10

Lee Harwood

Lee Harwood has been compared with the New York poets from whom he has learned, Frank O'Hara, John Ashbery, Kenneth Koch, and others, who have themselves learned from the abstract impressionist painters. What is common to all is the use of the elements of the medium, words or pigment, abstractly for evocation.[1] One may say of Harwood, especially of his later work, what Harold Rosenberg says of the painters: that the canvas appeared "as an arena in which to act—rather than as a space in which to reproduce. . . . What was to go on the canvas was not a picture but an event."[2] The poems in *Landscapes*, Harwood using painterly terms and describing canvases, come closer to works of the painters than does his earliest poetry, in which he parades details in a collagelike succession, as do the New Yorkers. But the details are not those

---

Lee Harwood (b. 1939 in Leicester) grew up in Chertsey (Surrey), and later in east London. He graduated from Queen Mary College, University of London, with a BA Honours degree in English in 1961. Since 1963 he has edited several "little magazines" and given poetry readings in England, the United States, France, Denmark, and Greece. Harwood has worked as a monumental mason, librarian, bookseller, forester, bus conductor, and currently works as a post office clerk. His home has been in Brighton (Sussex) since 1967, although from 1971 to 1972 he was writer-in-residence at the Aegean School of Fine Arts, Paros, Greece. Harwood received the Poets Foundation (New York) award in 1967 and the 1976 Alice Hunt Bartlett Prize (Poetry Society, London).

phenomena of city life as seen, for example, in O'Hara—
Madison Avenue, the bank, the subway, newspaper ven-
dors, apartment doorways, and endless others; Harwood's
details are derived from uncertain sources, often rural
scenes, small town or littoral, shards from memory, or
fragments of melodrama. James Schuyler says the New
York poets "are affected most by the floods of paint in
whose crashing surf we all scramble";[3] he would hardly
have spoken thus about Harwood in the early poems, in
which we are more conscious of mood spilling over than
of mere pigment or its equivalent. John Ashbery finds in
these poems a "pearly soft focus"; and there is a fundamental difference between his own dream poem, "The In-
struction Manual," and the dreamy poetry of the early
Harwood. Ashbery's is specifically a daydream: facing the
duty of writing the manual, the poet stares out of the window and imaginatively creates a vivid series of clear-cut
images of Guadalajara. A figure in a Harwood poem says,
"I will call anything that goes on in my head 'a dream,'
whether it be thoughts or imaginings, daydreams or sleep
dreams. They all give pictures of 'the possible,' and that is
exactly their value."[4] By comparison with Ashbery's poem,
however, Harwood's is more dreamy: in "When the Geography Was Fixed," for example, from *The White Room*, there
was a picture, and it was in a gallery. But it was really all to
do with this woman.

> The canvas is so bare
> that it hardly exists—though the painting
> is quite ready for the gallery opening.
> The clear droplets of water sparkle
> and the orange-red cloud hangs quite seductively.
> There is only one woman in the gallery now
> who knows what's really happening on the canvas—
> but she knew that already, and she
> also instinctively avoided all explanations.

All the same, in spite of factors that distinguish him, Harwood may be spoken of as instructed by Ashbery, who taught him, among other things, that a poem is an object, something made, like a good box.[5] Strong influences on his work came also from Tristan Tzara, the works and the man (whom he visited), and the French surrealists.

Most of Harwood's poems are about love, erotic or otherwise, but the theme is at the center of a circle where the poem, dwelling on the circumference, does not repeatedly look. Quite often, love is expressed directly in a mere word, in quotes though not necessarily speech, or as a banal word—as in these examples from *Landscapes*: "I love you"; "Gosh I do love you"[6]—sometimes the merest sliver of a phrase, almost of no account, almost overlooked. In literature, generally, love like any other passion becomes lodged in physical or natural objects. In Harwood's earliest poems, the relationship may be almost explicit, as in "When I See You Again":

> without you
> my star roams hungry
> a confusion of galaxies
> my charts don't work anymore.[7]

But later the relationship between the passion and the correlative physical object is unspoken; there is characteristically a gap, moreover, between the theme, blandly stated, and the texture of images upon which we are invited to spend most of our contemplation. Images gather according to two main forms in the earlier work: in "HMS Blue Flag,"[8] *The White Room*, and *The Sinking Colony*, the narrative; in *Landscapes*, the painting. But both narratives and paintings are incomplete, and form is not so remarkable as the freedom and spontaneity of surrealist creation.

Although details may be considerably more sharp edged than those in "When the Geography Was Fixed," Harwood is apparently bent in these volumes upon the expression of the life of the mind and not so much that of the external phenomenal world. Details from the world are his curious means toward that end: they may to some extent embody the life of the mind, or they may appear as witnesses of it and being such may be irradiated by it. A passage in *HMS Little Fox* is characteristic: the poet details a scene, then concludes the paragraph with this: "You melt into this landscape / and this only a description of my love for you."[9] In "Cable Street," he relates the external world to his consciousness of his love:

> I turn on and then re-read your poems. a fly buzzing round the wall and room centre. the mystery of stains at the bottom of a glass. eye slowly swivelling round. yet so soon I'm lost in your world as I read. the room is gone and all your words and pictures fill my head. and look out the window—children playing games in the school yard. the factory girls sunning themselves. their hair and breast obscured by white overalls. man eternally repairing his car—just the sound of his hammer striking the metal. so loud and important. pigeons swaying in the tree tops.[10]

Sometimes external and internal worlds are blended; in the train, he says,

> I put down the book and carefully poured another cup of
> tea
> avoiding spilling any
> . . . .
> The churchman was not so successful
> but his minor irritation was only passing
> I couldn't help but love him for this
> and it seemed a reflection of my love for you.[11]

Symbol and reality blend again in the title poem of *Landscapes*, which closes as follows:

The saddles creak & it's almost dusk.
It doesn't really matter whether this is
the real or a symbol—the end's the same.

"Telescope," also in *Landscapes*, presents an image of the sunlight, leading to the poet's response to the perception.

The comparison expands & I see this all as a
reflection of your coming return that I now wait for.
. . . .
Far from the shore a small cargo boat presses on
. . . .
. . . neither I nor the boat's crew
can be ruffled with such good things so obviously in store
for us.

In the story "Machines," the sentimentality of the subjective state recorded in quotation marks is intensified by the juxtaposition of the sight of quotidian rural work:

"breaking down at the continual brutality of it all, and my failure, once again. The tears flow down my face. I bury my head in the arms of the woman I've also failed."

A mile and a quarter walk away a black farm raincoat lies neatly folded up beside a tall hedge with a sharpening stone and bill hook laid on top of it.[12]

The relationships between the external and internal worlds are too complex and too shifting to be frozen as mere "objective correlative." The details in the broken narratives and the vague landscapes are presumably shadows of a psychic drama, not necessarily all of the same order of relatedness. The poet is looking for public details that will express, throw light on, or, on the other hand, momentarily distract him from the love business or some other activity of the mind. The objective parts of the poems must be considered not as settled embodiments, constituting a formula for this or that emotion, but as a heuristic: the poet tries things out; the texture of the poem is expendable. He suggests that it may be tone of voice rather than meanings of words that is significant. As he writes in "The Blue Mosque," "The facts and words—even whole lines— / could so easily be seen as matters of pure style."[13] A poem has the status of an artist's sketch, and in its failure to add up to a coherent story or picture it is the same kind of oddity as one of Leonardo's preliminary sketches in which a child may have, for example, two left arms. But to suggest that Harwood is looking for public details to relate to private sensations or that he uses external phenomena gives perhaps too strong an idea of the deliberateness in his procedure. Much of his work, recent work especially, is the product of an act done gratuitously: Harwood writes because it is his nature to make. His poems may be a bit like the machine in the story "Machines"—shiny on a mahogany base, with perfectly articulating parts performing no function at all.

The poems do not exist in his mind before they appear on paper; their shape comes as a novelty to Harwood. Repeatedly he jettisons details as unimportant after they have been presented; or he forcibly shifts us away from them by an ironic comment. "This already begins to sound like a very bad boy's story," he declares, two thirds of the way through "The Doomed Fleet";[14] in "When the Geography Was Fixed," Harwood tells us that "formality is just a cover." There are other throwaway lines and passages, such as "What else happened was forgotten" and

> This preoccupation with words can only be boring
> for the onlooker . . .
> . . . .
> What have any of these words to do with
> praising a good man or a love?[15]

"This is clumsy," a prose poem concludes,

but like a mould made to hold the final object
and then be destroyed or forgotten once the real
purpose was achieved—though such neatness in
explanation is always suspect.[16]

The feature common to all the poems and apparently of
fundamental importance to Harwood is inconclusiveness:
the incomplete narrative, the vague or incomplete picture.
He describes how he was moved by Constable and Moreau, recalling with enthusiasm a "terrific" picture by the
latter, "his finest," which is unfinished. "There are areas in
this canvas that are very elaborate in detail and others
which are left blank."[17] Harwood's own practice of inconclusiveness reflects openness: "The poem is always unfinished and open ended," he says in a note on the dust
jacket of *Landscapes*. His strategy of dissolving forms fulfills his aim to avoid fixed and final statements; these he
tends to use in quotation, with the understanding presumably that words generalize, are agents of distortion,
and thus are to be endlessly qualified by the texture of the
poems. Or statements may be used ironically: of the crowd
of spectators in "Central Park Zoo," he writes as if addressing himself to the schoolroom,

> some laugh with "joy", others gasp with "wonder"
> Let's call this charming story "A day at the zoo"—
> all essays to be handed in by the end of the week.[18]

In the same poem, he mulls over a decision—and avoids
making it, thereby averting the finality of closure.

> In fact let's forget what we'll call this
> Instead let's . . . returning to
> The zoo in the corner of the park
> the white mist hanging over the trees.

Harwood's firm commitment to uncertainty is sometimes reminiscent of Wallace Stevens and the poems that

reveal the endless flux. "The Final Painting" offers one example

> —nothing is limited by the canvas or frame—
> the white cloud can be pictured like any
> other clouds or like a fist of wool
> or a white fur rose.[19]

This passage suggests a conception of reality as ultimately indefinable, like the shifting visions of it in Stevens. As Harwood says in another poem collected in *Landscapes*, "Formal Portrait," "The number of possible scenes & descriptions / seems nearly as unlimited as the ever changing light."

The uncertainty is applied specifically in a later piece, "Old Bosham Bird Watch."[20] The nine vignettes that make up this "story" present scenes of the Sussex coast (Bosham is an old coastal parish in Sussex) and details of the simple life set there: ships, birds, preparing meals, and other routine items and events. These can be known. Among such firm particulars, however, Harwood expresses his sense of separation from knowledge of what is not established "like old photos making everything so set, clear, and easily understood." We do not know one another, including the beloved: "The sky, the gulls wheeling and squawking above the flint walls of these South Saxon churches, the yew trees branching up into the winter sky. I know these. But not what you're thinking, what anyone is thinking. I can never know that, only work with that—as it comes. Open arms open air come clear." Of what he does not know, however, he is not prepared to be exactly silent: simply by their propinquity, the qualities of the details of the known scene are bestowed on the unknown beloved—bestowed for both the reader and for the poet in his heuristic exercise.

Many poems in *The White Room* manifest two levels: on one hand there is a narrative; on the other, passages in quotation that speak more or less directly to a theme. The narratives often contain images from the medieval world, especially of knights and horsemen, accompanying contemporary images in the same poem. Quite frequently, there are images or terms that elevate the speaker: he becomes a nobleman or the strongman of a banana republic or has at least some rank from which he gives orders, satisfying perhaps a need for grandeur. The narrative details are often melodramatic, and they are always fragmentary. They remind us of the early Auden, in the war games poems, when he has "seen the last of Captain Ferguson" or is to "Leave for Cape Wrath tonight"—because the details lack explanatory context, they have some mystery and magic about them (if we knew what was going to happen to Captain Ferguson or the reason for going to the Cape we would be less impressed). The narrative details in Harwood's early poems are similarly mysterious because they are fragmentary and unexplained and to that extent powerful. In "The Doomed Fleet," for example, the following unrelated news is offered:

> The wounded was a subject never touched on
> in the officers' mess. And the question of
> occasional small but brutal outbreaks of
> disease was similarly treated.[21]

In "Goodbye Tom,"

> The radio plays more music, though it is the
> soldiers in the castle who select the dance records
> and the nature of the provisions is still a secret.[22]

It remains so.

Most often we do not know how the vivid details of a narrative are to be ordered; there seems to be some vital footage missing in which the clues are contained. In *Landscapes*, we are faced with the same uncertainty, having no clear vision of the paintings that the poems half describe:

outlines of the landscapes are scumbled; colors alternately fade and intensify; only occasionally in the foreground there may be a few well-defined figures against the vague, shifting backdrop.

A closer look at some particular poems is worthwhile. From *The White Room*, "The Argentine" opens with references to a ranch and to its associated terrain. There are "wrong and arrogant statements" about the land in geography books resented by the poet. (*Geography* here and elsewhere, including "When the Geography Was Fixed," signifies what is complete and opposed to the openness that the poet desiderates.) Next, there are images of destruction—destruction by brown rivers and then by the poet himself who, looking for someone, "kicked every door down in the house." Horsemen appear and the poet leaves with them. In the meantime, the love theme has been introduced in a quoted whisper:

> "Can't you understand my difficulties?" was
> whispered as I put my ear to the ground
> "I wasn't prepared, and she could not wait
> for ever" the voice went on and on.

The second part of the poem refers to a journey, a frequent motif in the pseudonarrative poems. Part three introduces memories—of airport lounges, the bus terminal, and other details associated with an intimate relationship. When these memories grow unbearable, there are visits to other ranches. One or two details of a car trip follow; then,

> All this seized in weak desperation to distract
> a realisation, and sometimes even a regret
>
> Such an image had been set so deep in my heart
> that its destruction would inevitably cause
> much more than local damage
> and the fire chief didn't exaggerate when he said
> "keep all those people well clear. . . ."

The level of the poem at which the distraction and the destruction are to occur is not made clear—whether the actor in the melodrama is referring to details of the trip or the poet to the poem.

The fourth part describes how of three men parting on Fifth Avenue one of the two younger had kissed the older man and the third felt the frustration of a missed chance. This part concludes with a similar failure in a heterosexual relationship related in a torn letter found in a hotel room. Part five returns us to images of the ranch; the last part states that the "view from the mountain pass / suddenly made everything seem clear" and that "answers were obvious." The poem concludes as follows:

> The journey had to be made and the horsemen were right
> But the weight of possessions held onto,
> if not for love of them, then for some sense of duty
> and fear
>
> These accounts of past and future journeys
> became boring . . . and any violence that might have been
> had now grown limp like the vase of dead flowers
> that the efficient house-keeper will surely clear away

The summary gives some sense of the waywardness of the details, the sudden shifts in direction, as in the last passage quoted, following the breaking off of a statement in midsentence, and the manner in which, as in the previous quotation, subjective matters give way without warning to narrative that may or may not be a figure for them.

The source of the images in these poems is not given—there are no notes as there are, for instance, in Eliot, Beckett, Marianne Moore, Nathaniel Tarn, or Basil Bunting (tantalizing though some of these may be). The poems are probably not pure psychic automatism, though the images have no doubt come, with minimal editing, from beneath consciousness. Throughout there is travel—in the narratives particularly, but also in *Landscapes*—involving ships and cars, more often trains and horses. The journeys are represented as necessary, often sad; they may be quests; sometimes they seem to lead the traveler away from despair, helplessness, and terror, or, as in "The Argentine," from his own passions. After registering his discontent, resentment, and anger, the poet realizes

> It was opportune that at this moment
> the group of horsemen galloped into
> the court-yard,

knowing also, "I was prepared to ride away with them."

Whether as a surrealist poet he ought to be traveling away from passion is a good question, especially, as it happens, if he travels on horseback. Images of horsemen are frequent throughout the poems, and the speaker himself is often mounted. Jung has noted that the rider and horse form a centaurlike unit of ego-consciousness and shadow, and the horsemen in Harwood may thus symbolize the rational in control of the lower, irrational components of the mind. There is sometimes a quiet resignation in the acceptance of the role as horseman: in "The Journey," "It was strange—getting used to the rhythm of my / saddle again after the long period of inactivity"; in "The Argentine," "I was prepared to ride away with them." But the subjugation of the irrational part of his nature is crippling for a poet who depends for his work on the unfettered unconscious content. Thus it is not surprising that the appearance of the horsemen throughout the poems should be accompanied by apathy and listlessness or, indeed, that the horsemen should be associated with death. In one poem Harwood describes "The wood-cut of a lone horseman / riding through a deathly countryside."[23] Shortly after mounting in "The Journey," the poet announces the nearness of his death, and the prose poem concludes with a duel. In "Landscapes," the horsemen will ford "the shallow river," after which death is implied: "From then on it is not very far / to their destination. We both know this."

Concerning the incompleteness, the openness of his poetry, Harwood has remarked as follows:

> The poem is always unfinished and open ended and only complete (and then only in one way) when read by someone else. I mean a work of art which only achieves wholeness when an audience is present. . . . The important telegram torn in half and only one half given to the reader to fill in the missing half. That's what my poems are about. The reader fills in the blanks with his own memories and imaginations so each reader creates a different poem from the basic foundations the writer gives him.[24]

But it is hard to imagine that the poet, though he makes great imaginative demands on the reader, intends him to assemble the poem mechanically out of the given clues, as the telegram comparison suggests. The remark about Moreau's painting quoted above suggests a less mechanical activity of the reader: concerning the areas left blank, "You can spend hours in front of this canvas filling them in, and you aren't just filling them in on the picture, but your head is going out everywhere else, and your head affects your conduct." Nor is the reader to assemble any single construction; in "Question of Geography,"

> you paint over the picture & start on
> the new one   but all the same it's still there
> beneath the fresh plains of colour.[25]

The reader should perhaps disdain the false blandishments of narrative content and withstand the instinct to make a logical construction. As if by way of a corrective to his comment about the telegram, Harwood says,

> ——————————PLATO was right to banish
> poets from the Republic. Once they try to go beyond the
> colours and shapes, they only ever fail, miserably—
> some more gracefully than others.[26]

These are the last words in *The White Room*.

The pseudonarrative forms of *The White Room* are replaced in *Landscapes* by painting terms: there are fat tubes of paint, canvases and frames, perspective, and vivid color. One poem refers specifically to Constable's "Weymouth Bay," another to "The Emperor Shah Jahan," by Bichitra; another notes that

> The whole situation
> was like a painting within a painting &
> that within another & so on & so on.[27]

The incompleteness of the poems in *The White Room* that results from fragmentary detail and missing links comes in *Landscapes* from dissolving outlines, and the poems dwell repeatedly on bareness and whiteness. In "When the Geography Was Fixed," Harwood writes that "the colours are hard to name / since a whiteness infiltrates everything." In "Telescope,"

> A pale late winter sunshine floods the whole landscape
> in a harsh white light & so makes it
> look totally bare—the word "naked" can even be used
> now.

That whiteness is potential is clear in "Camels"—"through the large white window the sky's stretched out like / a canvas"—awaiting completion.

Landscapes are faded into whiteness in order that they may be painted anew, so that whiteness plays the same role as silence in Harwood's earliest work and in the work of certain other poets, such as Nathaniel Tarn. In "Quiet Love Song," the first poem of *The White Room*, silence cuts out the external world and provides a matrix for the expression of the inner life:

It is strange how in this quiet
for the first time
I hear my own voice
dark in the silence of this room.

In addition, silence may be the medium from which the
poet has relinquished his control, leaving it with infinite
possibility and assuring the poem of openness. Whiteness
in Harwood is a second development from the platitude of
the clichés: after the bland "I love you" comes the heuristic
action in a plenitude of pigment; after that, the bare canvas.

Harwood who loves contrasts, often shocking ones, de-
lights in the contrasts between action and background,
theme and texture, images of noise and the silence they
invade, or those of color against a blank matrix. In his earliest poems, rockets defeat the quiet; later, clouds of color
swirl through the watercolor water or clouds of dust swirl
across deserts. Sometimes against a soft landscape an image of a pistol or a plane is suddenly projected. Whiteness,
in line with this general predilection for contrasts, provides a ground for action.

From *Landscapes*, "Formal Portrait" shows the relationship between textural detail and the theme of love. It begins with a description of pictures: in one, "The Emperor
Shah Jahan is shown in his garden"; in another, "Ladies sit
delicately on the swings." After the descriptions and some
imaginative enlargement of the pictures, there is a modu-
lation into a present reality:

A mirror made of highly polished metal
I see your reflection in this & in myself
The moon shines too above the many seatowns strung
    along the coast
. . . .
In Kashmir & other Himalayan foothills
Bichitr the artist in "1663" came to see
you swim naked to the waist in "a lotus pond"—

> the hills behind the colour of a sliced blood-orange
> I watch you undisturbed—your neat firm breasts.

The poet has identified the "you," the person in the present, with the lady in the picture. He returns, next, to the lady of the swing, but now she comes in different settings—caught in a storm, and "At the tryst." Then,

> Sometimes you are the lady, but most often
> you are even more beautiful than she is
> or ever could be.

Finally,

> As you sleep the fine garden is deserted
> except for the moon & a few tigers
> The Emperor wears rich scarlet slippers
> as he stands beside the hollyhocks unnoticed
> Perhaps tonight he thinks of the war on the plains
> or remembers when his palace was eaten by fire
> You are quite safe & there is no worry.

The poem is a particular instance of a process that is generally at work in Harwood: a series of shifting images—the lady "delicately" swinging, then swimming, then hurrying in a storm—with a shifting, noncommittal relationship to the central love theme—"Sometimes you are the lady." "It is hard to know," says the poet, as he presents the various situations of the lady,

> It is hard to know if these are exercises in grammar
> or attempts at communication of sorts
> either by the painter or the lady maybe,

or, of course, the poet.

Harwood's more recent works, *Freighters* and parts of *HMS Little Fox*, present his observations in a structure even less binding than the melodramas and paintings of the earlier volumes. Moreover, the structure is spatial rather than linear, as far as these things may be. Of the first part of *HMS Little Fox*, "The Long Black Veil: a note-book *1970–72*," Harwood says that it not only contains "varied information" but has "an energy and necessity as well." A poem in twelve books, it is the "flower" of his work to date, he says.[28] The varied information includes landscapes—idyllic scenes mostly—records of times with his beloved, dreams, notes on his reading and quotations therefrom, and notes from visits to museums. Each page of book twelve is marked with an outline drawing of Hathor, the Egyptian goddess, who stands, we are told in the seventh book, for the sky, and thus presides over the peaceful ending of this poem. The poem is a clear example of the mosaic, nonlinear structure that Harwood has come to consider the only possible kind. "To make a poem of different fragments," he says, "was much more true and accurate to the world we live in than forcing the world into a two plus two equals four, or an A, B, C, D structure."[29] The end of the poem is about physical love and the rituals attending it, the passage gathering together and crowning the other separate instances of lovemaking throughout the poem.

"The Long Black Veil" opens with a contrasting pair of passages.

> How to accept
> this drift
>
> the move   not mapped
> nor clear other than in
> its existence,

A question followed a few lines later by a quotation:

> "Concepts promise protection
> from experience.
> The spirit does
> not dwell in concepts. Oh Jung."

The meaning of Harwood's claim that the poem has energy is not entirely clear; it may be that he thinks of it as an "energy construct," Charles Olson's term, which is likewise not entirely clear. Possibly the way to "accept this drift" is to conceive of the energy as tension deriving from the love passages, the positive poles, set against the abstract concepts embodied in the quotations from books and references to museums, the negative poles—a system like the yin yang, which appears in a diagram at one point in the poem. The tension between these two categories of interest is not very remarkable, however, although toward the end of the poem there is this observation:

> when we're together the time always so short. The
> minutes counted and noted down. And around these
> times the long hours of waiting.

As "The Long Black Veil" alternates between these two categories of elements, so *Freighters*, a shorter poem published as a book in 1975, alternates between details of the poet's private life, his memories, and local scenes on the one hand and documentary details about the Sussex coast and its shipping on the other. It is a mosaic. The former parts are in poetry; they list things or describe the poet being tired at evening, preparing meals, listening to the radio, reading, playing with his cats, and so on. The passage of poetry that ends the book introduces his lover; there are freighters on the horizon, but he feels

> the pain—yes—a knife hacks
>   stabs, and cuts deep
> I know
> but your sweet smiling face
>   making all clear
>   and exciting.

The context of the poetry—the other parts of the book—consists of maps, geological diagrams of increasing complexity, press clippings about shipping, and passages from local guide books (not verbatim) describing topology, the dates of churches, cargoes of ships, the silting up of rivers, and the gradual drift of the ports as they move inland. It is tempting to describe the poem as an answer to *The Anath-émata* "with the bare hands"—whereas David Jones finds that all things, even the geology of Great Britain, point to the Christian mystery, Lee Harwood finds that it is all a context for his own private self—the quotidian self with a job, the daily chores, and a love life. More properly the work should be related to that of Charles Olson. It is the nearest work in Britain to the *Maximus* poems: both have departed without compromise from the tradition, rejecting conventional form, substituting mosaic for discourse. Harwood, like Maximus, relates himself to the geography of a port, concerned with shipping and history.

11

Tom Raworth

There are poems in Raworth of one word or two, or a single word repeated, or a title with nothing following it; there is a poem in which a drawing of a pencil underlines a single quotation from Ezra Pound, and poems where the print is crossed out and simulated cursive is substituted. One's response to such work is guarded by the recollection of two notable responses in the past: Sir John Squire's to *The Waste Land*, "A grunt would have served as well," and the public's response to the ready-mades of Marcel Duchamp, who remarks in a letter to Hans Richter, "I threw the bottle rack and the urinal in their faces as a challenge and now they admire them for their aesthetic beauty."[1]

It has been suggested that art is an opportunity for its audiences to experience the inherent disorder of the world, that reality has no form and no continuity, but in everyday living it is denatured, selected, and ordered in the very act

---

Tom Raworth (b. 1938) is a poet, novelist, and translator. Between 1959 and 1967 he edited, printed, and published the magazine *Outburst* (London), ran Matrix Press, and, with Barry Hall, founded Goliard Press. Like many contemporary poets, Raworth has at times been linked with higher education, having taught or been poet-in-residence at universities in Britain and the United States: Essex (1969–1970); Bowling Green, Ohio (1972–1973); Northeastern Illinois, in Chicago (1973–1974); Texas, at Austin (1974–1975); and King's College, Cambridge (1977–1978). At other times he has been a clerk, laborer, switchboard operator, packer of underground comics, guinea pig for eye research, and unemployed.

of perception itself. Art, however, conditions one to see, outside the framework of customary orientation, reality's irrelevant texture.[2] The idea comes to mind in a consideration of Raworth's earliest volume, *The Relation Ship*. In "Six Days," a six-part sequence, are assembled details of the experience of a week; they are not selected according to logic or narrative, nor are they directed toward usefulness or pointed toward a theme. As Raworth has declared elsewhere, they are real details from real life during a week in Paris, jotted down on scraps of paper.[3] These lines are from "wednesday":

> i have no love and therefore i have liberty it said on the
> wall and underneath with my key i scratched "lincoln"
> pas lincoln she said bien sûr i answered an elastic band
> floated by
> there are statues of all the queens of france she said there
> was cream on her nose
>
> my throat is sore do not go down those alleys at night
> there are thieves and murderers
> this cinema is the biggest in europe maurice thorez est
> mort enregistrez un disque a way to send letters.

Charles Olson praised *The Relation Ship* as "preternaturally wise," and, indeed, many of its poems act in accordance with Olson's precepts for projective verse. The poems move from one perception to another, avoiding description; Raworth, like Olson, is concerned with the energy in the poem, energy that may determine its shaping.[4] Similarly, Raworth's poems often demonstrate the pure objectivity and the absence of imposed structure as prescribed by Olson: "The objects which occur at every given moment of composition (of recognition, we can call it) are, can be, must be treated exactly as they do occur therein and not by any ideas or preconceptions from outside the poem, must be handled as a series of objects in field."[5]

In the paucity of its use of any kind of adjective, and the

complete absence of any gratuitous one, and in its innocence of any predetermined theme or predetermined pattern, the "Six Days" sequence and many of Raworth's other
poems reflect the precepts and the styles of the Black
Mountain poets. But although he knew Olson and en-
joyed conversation with him, and although his interest
in jazz had led him to read Ginsberg, and Ed Dorn had
started him writing, he is not necessarily anyone's disciple
or student. He veers deliberately from influence, as does
Roy Fisher; indeed, Gael Turnbull's comment on Fisher's
City might be made of the poems of Raworth: "in the hap-
pening of an action, all that can be willed is to give oneself
as fully as possible to what is going on, to try above all to
be true to the closest instinct of the moment, at each moment. Even when its pattern or its meaning may appear
utterly lost."[6] In "Six Days," in almost all Raworth's poems
in fact, pattern is lost, successfully lost—but not necessarily coherence, of which something is gained in the urgency
with which one detail presses forward upon the next. The
urgency is cultivated, resulting, for instance, from the
position of the "i" before the line break in two lines from
"Six Days"—

> my hair in a window in the tube it was still summer i
> was and still am addicted to self-pity

—thus separating subject from verb is "the only way to
keep the speed going," Raworth remarks.[7] The details of
"Six Days," boring though they may be in life itself, are
here recorded and, thus set apart, gain the kind of attention paid, say, to a fragment of hessian in an abstract collage, a bit of driftwood set on polished mahogany, or a
ready-made of Duchamp. "With a child's hand," says a reviewer, "he picks up pieces of language rubbish and turns
on them a child's almost muscular powers of appropria-
tion."[8] One motive for the recording of detail is release. (It

is a "release to write it down," says the narrator in *A Serial Biography*, an assemblage constructed of letters from Raworth to Ed Dorn and additional prose, presenting anecdotes from the lives of some eight or nine characters derived from the associative memory of the narrator. In certain Kafkaesque parts of the book, the narrator is incarcerated in a dark room within a room, the object of an experiment being performed on him by unknown though not entirely hostile persons designated "they"; at other times, he sits at a typewriter, accurately recording the objects within his range of vision.) Generally, however, the details of "Six Days" do not serve a local purpose and receive more attention than if they did; released from context like the images in Hollo, they are more vivid than they would be in conventional frameworks.

The details are not ironic. In "Six Days," Raworth is demonstrating the richness of a day, not its triviality. Nor is he ironic in another poem when, having assumed the most undignified posture available to mortals, he records what he sees, as if, like the artist Richard Hamilton, he were searching for what is epic in everyday objects and everyday attitudes:

> the shadows, medicines, a wicker
> laundry basket lid pink with toothpaste
>
> between my legs i read
>   levi stra
>   origina
>   quality clo
>   leaning too far forward
> into the patch of sunlight[9]

A reviewer complains that Raworth's "short-winded jottings" masquerade as epiphanies.[10] They certainly serve to cleanse the phenomenal world of its film of custom, the habitualization that, according to Victor Shklovsky, "devours objects, clothes, furniture, one's wife, and the fear of war,"[11] inspiring us to say, "O brave new world that has such toothpaste in it!"

Vividness is a regular quality of Raworth's images, as these examples from *The Relation Ship* will show: "the land of animals & hot wet leaves," in "She Said Bread, Fred"; "handkerchief caught in a branch / waiting for a stronger wind," in "The Third Retainer"; "in the ashtray an apple core a / spoon with milk skin," in "For Paul Dorn"; "the phone ringing in the empty house," in "There are Lime Trees in Leaf on the Promenade." All these things, which in life are often and routinely experienced, are now sharp in the mind.

In the assembly of a poem, Raworth makes no distinction between images and events of present experience and those in memory. Sometimes the coalescence of present and past is the main feature, the point, one may say, of a poem. In *The Relation Ship*, "The Blood Thinks, and Pauses" opens with the poet and "you" talking, as they sit in a train stopped on the bridge over the Menai Strait on a calm day with gulls. He is thinking among other things of an occasion many years before when he ate his first peach and sucked the stone dry. He thinks also of the remark of a poet (or perhaps an editor). As the poem ends,

> i had been talking to you
>   thinking this and other
> things
>   he wants, he had said
> a poetry of violence   gulls
> dropped
>   looking for peach stones

Fact, thought, and memory are compacted as being of a single order. So too are fact and imagination in "The Wall," when the poet as a continental telephone operator constructs a minor drama on the basis of fragments heard on the wire:

> it is cold
> i hold her hand in my pocket
> . . . .
> a single car
> is parked in the square. *now*
> i can understand all she's saying.[12]

Or, in "Hot Day at the Races," the products of familiar observation are inextricably entangled with those of wild imagination.

> shelley is waiting with a crossbow for his rival, the jockey
> all day he's watched the races from his bush
> now, with eight and a half furlongs to go
> raw silk at least four lengths back disputing third place
> he takes aim.[13]

Throughout Raworth there are phrases, sometimes clichés, self-consciously pointed to as phrases, rather as Henry James in his quite different world draws attention to words as words by his use of quotation marks. Raworth may or may not use such marks; he may present phrases entirely without context. He writes, for example, "'He speaks for all of us'"[14] and "'they're the gentlest of animals, koala bears.'"[15] Sometimes the phrases are explicitly pointed to: "The dust on the hem of her blue gown / blue gown—that's nice";[16] "bitter moon dances a phrase we overheard."[17] Raworth can say, "there's nothing wrong with it really   i / inhabit a place just to the left of that phrase."[18]

The image of the phone ringing in the empty house is taken from a poem in *The Relation Ship* and is somewhat atypical in that many of its images and events, while they are presented as autonomous, point to a theme, though this is not actually stated, either directly or obliquely. Like many of Raworth's, the title, "There are Lime Trees in Leaf on the Promenade," though it announces springtime, bears little manifest relation to the poem, which commences with the image of a blossom blowing across a step and proceeds to describe the celebration for the twentieth anniversary of the World War II victory in Paris—fireworks, parades, and this:

> all across the town the signs the french
> people are not your allies mr. johnson.

Shortly,

> we came
> separately home
> the children were there
> covered with pink blossoms like burned men.

The image relates to the passage about Johnson and thus the Vietnam War. After a few lines there follow these, which suggest that cruelty prevails in nature.

> swans
> built their nests behind the lockgates   the eggs
> when the gates were opened
> smashed.   each time in pairs the swans
> would hunt out ducklings, and whilst one
> held off the mother, would drown them
> beating them under the water with their wings.

Next Raworth presents the image of the telephone ringing, and then at last the poet quotes from Sun Tzu:

> " . . . a kingdom
> that once has been destroyed
> can never come again into being; nor can the dead
> ever be brought back to life.   hence the enlightened ruler
> is heedful, and the good general full of caution."

The poem plays about the theme of the war: it begins with victory and closes with defeat. And once the theme is suggested, the strange natural history of the swans can be clearly seen as contributing to the overall effect.

In the sequence "Stag Skull Mounted,"[19] a theme is vaguely approached in another way, enacted rather than expressed. As the occasion of the opening poem, Raworth has described how he and a friend saw a bare skull nailed through the eye sockets to the wall of a pub: "They really wanted it, or liked it, to be dead: to be that sure."[20] The poem addresses itself to the smallness of mankind:

> mounting a stag's skull remains
> the province of a tiny man
> who standing on a bolt peers
> across eye socket rim at antlers.

In the second poem, the poet expresses his own worthlessness at the thought of projecting his own sadness onto a crippled girl:

> the weight
> of my thought of her misery may add
> the grain that makes her sad   i should be dead

The main but not the exclusive business of this sequence (images arising from the hashish the poet has eaten are also included) is the enactment of self-abnegation: we witness the progressive emptying of language from the mind, the mind reducing itself to a single word and from that to vacancy, with the prospect, which proves to be vain, of beginning again out of ignorance to create anew. The times and dates of impulses that become the poems forming the sequence are given as titles. The poems, says Raworth, are "in some way the explanations and contradictions of those particular moments."[21] "NOON MAY 29th. 1970" begins,

> i can not find my way
> back to myself i go
> on trying

"1.31 PM. JUNE 5th. 1970" opens thus:

> my up
> is mind made
>
> absolutely empty

At 10.26 on 5 June, all that was there in the way of impulse was the word *word*. At 10.59, same day, there was nothing, and the page is blank. At 10.45 the morning of the following day, the poet looked up *word* in a dictionary—the act of renewal—and thought, "how would you look it up if you didn't know anything, just the shape. You look up 'word' and the first word of that definition is also 'the.' You're stuck. There's nothing you can do." [22] The word that came at 8.06 P.M., 10 June, was *poem*, which, says Raworth, "fulfills every dictionary definition of a poem except that poems sometimes rhyme. So the next one, later on that evening, was obviously 'poem / poem.' No one can fault that as a poem by any 'definition.' And then, yeah, on to the end of that." [23] But "the end of that" seems to have been a failure: "7.40 PM. JUNE 29th. 1970" reads, "this trick doesn't work."

Occasionally among Raworth's poems there may be one in which the imagery swirls obsessively about a single thing: "Gitanes" returns continuously to cigarette butts, "Shoes" to shoes. [24] Of most of the poems, however, if there is a paradigm controlling images and events, it is too vague for our apprehension. The epigraph to *The Relation Ship*, taken from "Buckingham Palace" by Piero Heliczer, instructs us that "Babies grow filling out a shape without having been dropped in a mould"; the poem "Wedding Day" in the same volume makes the Bergsonian assertion that "i made this pact, intelligence / *shall* not replace intuition."

In a number of poems, the deployment of events comes near the expression of an emotion. Sometimes the happenings and assemblages of artists, constructed purely for the sake of the rhythm of events and objects, have been discerned on reflection to address a theme. A poem of Raworth's is often like an assemblage: items in unusual contexts or not strictly in any context shine into being; they may or may not subscribe to a unity. In *Big Green Day*, "North Africa Breakdown" is an example of a poem in which disparate items seem to point incidentally and uncertainly toward the expression of feeling.

> it was my desert army. no fuss. no incidents.
> you just have to be patient with it. take your time.
> a child leaving a dirty black car (with running boards)
> wearing a thick too large overcoat: grainy picture.
> each night round the orange dial of the wireless.
>
> or innocence. oh renaissance.
> a dutch island where horses pull to launch the lifeboat.
> we are specifically ordered that there shall be no fast cars.
> where can we go when we retire?
>
> it was their deduction we were afraid of
> so shall we try just once more?
> nothing is too drastic when it comes to your son, eleanor.
>
> and nothing works in this damn country.
> no, it's not a bit like home.

The last two lines suggest alienation. What the poet is alienated from is his childhood, when the desert army was "his" (he must have been about six or seven when the Eighth Army was chasing Rommel across Libya), when there were cars with running boards, and the family gathered round the radio at night. The safe, withdrawn world is identified with both childhood and retirement: as men look back to an Eden lost, they look forward to a second Eden earned, the poet anticipating withdrawal to innocence, a primitive Dutch island "where horses pull to launch the lifeboat."

The poem's opening fiction—"my desert army," whether

toys or not—is a familiar feature. Raworth repeatedly shifts his reader into a childhood world of toys or imagination:

> snow falling on the lemon trees
> the cowboy shivering in his saddle
> what patience required to make *models*![25]

Like Roy Fisher, Raworth is liable to take a curious angle of vision to gain a new slant on familiar phenomena, as in the bathroom poem or in "What is the Question":

> a car is approaching my left eye sees it reflected filling half
>   a lens
> and all out*side* the rim is black.[26]

These are small tactics in a general strategy of unfocusing. What Edward Lucie-Smith remarks of unfocusing in painting may be applied to Raworth's poetry: "The artist does not create something separate and closed, but instead does something to make the spectator more open, more aware of himself and his environment."[27] The comment can be applied particularly to those poems in which the poet employs silence or the rests in his jazz rhythms and invites the reader's entry. "Sing," for example, from *The Relation Ship*, begins,

> a certain
> drum beat   it is that of
> skin
>
> the button found
> still
>   vibrating
>
> produce
> the body.

Scope for imaginative creation by the reader comes through the ellipses. John Cage has observed that sounds that are not notated "appear in the written music as silences opening the doors of the music to the sounds that happen to be in the environment."[28] The poem, on the other hand, is opened to the more personal images and ideas that appear to the individual reader as the words are momentarily unharnessed. It calls, as Raworth's later poems increasingly call, for the reader's completion.

In his volume *Act*, Raworth has pared away the flesh of the poems until what is left is a mere skeleton. If in earlier work he was unwilling to come to focus with a direct expression, here he has reduced poetry to the merest nervous mutterings. "Situations," for example, runs as follows:

> inside
> the pantomime horse
>
> a door in the t.v. opened
> i felt the draught
>
> colonel
> eternal

This is the product of an instinct common to a number of modern poets (and painters too, in their own way) who, reacting against the danger of saying too much, come out tight-lipped and minimal. Published in the same year as *Act*, the following poem, titled "NO PEACE / BLACK HOLES / EARTH CRACKS," both expresses the point and demonstrates it.

> there's a lot of things you can do
> without using words—i was doing i
> very hungry. the red elastic mark.[29]

In the earlier work and in this brief poem, Raworth makes a personal poetic idiom out of detail unsupplied with context. Sometimes individual words, rather than an isolated image or act, are the units of his idiom. His use recalls the condition of words in modern poetry as Roland Barthes celebrates it: "In classical speech, connections lead the word on, and at once carry it towards a meaning which is an ever-deferred project; in modern poetry, connections are only an extension of the word, it is the Word which is 'the dwelling place.' . . . it is the Word which gratifies and fulfills like the sudden revelation of a truth." [30] Indeed, Raworth pays homage in recent volumes to the single word; "Star Rats," from *Act*, for example, opens thus:

moon
rust
train

Further pulling away from meanings but not quite detached from them, Raworth lays emphasis on their sounds. "Olive Mandate" begins,

good luck jim olive mandate
takes top prize for every thing olive mandate
that the interest is changing forms olive mandate. [31]

Or he may exploit the visual effects of words in the manner of concrete poetry. "Your Slip's Showing," for instance, closes,

m o o n
   o
m o o d
   e [32]

It is, of course, clever and relatively new. The mirror game is also clever:

sun leaves the leaves
send this and strawberry
chewing gum to aram

mara ot *mug* gniwehc
yrrebwarts *dna* siht dnes
sevael eht sevael nus [33]

—an allusion to Aram Saroyan and his child Strawberry. Cuteness produces amusement, but the performance does not disturb the whole mind, totally engaged. If we believe David Jones's contention that art settles to the level of what we believe, such recent minimal productions should give us pause.

12

Conclusion

The exhibition of Tom Raworth's unfleshed poems is a reasonable point at which to terminate this sampling of contemporary or recent British poets—each conventionally independent, doing his own unconventional thing; each also, willy-nilly, the product of his/time and place. All show American influence: Roy Fisher the least; Harwood, Hollo, and Raworth, the heaviest; and Tomlinson, whose work is closest of all to the tradition, the most varied. And all show concern with the poem's role as a mirror of the real or with its absolute autonomy as a thing in itself.

Much contemporary English poetry, like much contemporary American, is open poetry—the term strictly an oxymoron, since the openness precludes the fashioning implicit in *poetry*. Traditionally, all the arts sought to deliver a world supported by universally attractive formal features, a golden world in Sir Philip Sidney's phrase. In the work of Tomlinson and the early Hughes are poems that reflect parts of a recognizable world in formally closed units. In most of the poets discussed above, however, the world is presented in a poetry for which structural support has not been scrupulously sought or has been actively avoided.

In discussing the anti-novel, Frank Kermode said, "Even when there is a profession of complete narrative anarchy, as . . . in a poem such as *Paterson*, which rejects as spurious whatever most of us understand as form, it seems that time will always reveal some congruence with a paradigm—provided always that there is in the work that necessary element of the customary, which enables it to communicate at all."[1] The revelations of time, of course, are in fact the product of the creative intelligence of readers, whose contribution in the making of art Kermode recognizes. But the cultivated anarchy of much contemporary verse taxes the mind beyond its ordering ability: we may scrutinize the words in Geoffrey Hill for overtones in etymology and elsewhere, and we may recreate his paradigms; in other poets, not so. Harwood, for example, seems to resist such intelligent work (despite the claim that the poem is like a torn telegram), moving the reader on from one image to the next, claiming that his verse fragments are "more true and accurate" to our world than a structured poem. Some things of Raworth's are likewise forbidding to the ordering mind.

It may be claimed that such work does not, all the same, defy Kermode's principle: in short, it fails to reveal pattern because it lacks the "necessary element of the customary" and thus fails to communicate. The judgment would not be unduly harsh for some adventitious contemporary jottings that have, temporarily at least, fooled the reading public, but it may not be applied where the poet has deliberately avoided reference and sought for his work an independence from the world. The cubists contrived to enforce the reading of their works as colored canvases and not illusions of reality; so some contemporary poets, like Bunting and Fisher, for example, have not necessarily precluded the reader from discovery of a paradigm, despite fighting off, to some extent, meaning.

The loss of structure in art means a loss of frame, the line that separates it from other things. Allan Kaprow says that the bison in the cave existed in no space except the space within the animal's outline. "When next a horizon line was drawn under a cow, the separation of image from environment occurred like a logical thunderbolt, and thereafter painting (and man) could never be the same. Painting had become symbol rather than power, i.e., something which *stood for* experience rather than *acting directly upon it*."[2] In all the arts there are now reversions to the frameless condition: works break out, usurping the prerogatives of life itself, its heterogeneity, its incoherence, its inconclusiveness, and often enough, alas, its dullness. Painting moves out of its two dimensions into the living space; sculpture is exhibited out of doors to escape the framework of the gallery; ballet choreographies are opened up to accommodate idiosyncrasies; drama advances across the proscenium to bring the audience into the act—the person sitting next to you turns out to be a part of the cast, as without knowing it you may be yourself; a harpsichord piece runs off the end of the keyboard to be drummed out on the wood; orchestral works are uncaged of their structures; plastic art is unfrozen to become the mobile; the plotted film is replaced by the lusterless documentary or the mere sequence of one damn thing after another, events vivid enough, but with no organized prevailing direction visible. These arts, then, and open poetry also, may be thought of not as reflections but as experience itself, acting directly on experience, a part of life. In 1927, but with a curiously contemporary ring, Jane Harrison wrote, "Art . . . goes back as it were on her own steps, recrossing the ritual bridge back to life."[3] By no means nowadays is poetry necessarily "already lived experience," Auden's phrase for it in the *New Year Letter*, crafted into form. And D. H. Lawrence might have been speaking of much contemporary work when he said, "There is no static perfection, none of that finality which we find so satisfying because we are so frightened."[4] And behind such artless poetry, unprotected by any refracting medium, stands the poet, manifestly present, without guile—his taste, his vision, his voice—alone in the dispossessed world, surveying fragments of it without trying to set it in order, or determined, in his avoidance of a structure, to recognize its inhuman otherness, knowing only that it is there.

Notes

Notes to Chapter 1:
Introduction

1. John Matthias, ed., *23 Modern British Poets* (Chicago: Swallow Press, 1971).
2. Marjorie Perloff, "The Two Poetries: An Introduction," *Contemporary Literature* 18 (Summer 1977): 264.
3. Denise Levertov, "An English Event," *Kulchur* 2 (Summer 1962): 3.
4. Donald Davie, "See and Believe," review of Charles Tomlinson's *Seeing is Believing*, in *The Poet in the Imaginary Museum* (Manchester: Carcanet, 1977), 67.
5. Ekbert Faas, "Ted Hughes and Crow," *London Magazine*, n.s., 10 (January 1971): 10–11.
6. A. R. Jones, "Necessity and Freedom," *Critical Quarterly* 7 (Spring 1965): 11.
7. Henri Chopin, "Why I Am the Author of Sound Poetry and Free Poetry," trans. Irene Montjoye Sinor and Mary Ellen Solt, in *Concrete Poetry: A World View*, ed. Mary Ellen Solt (Bloomington: Indiana University Press, 1968), 80.
8. In a statement for the BBC, quoted in M. L. Rosenthal, "Olson / His Poetry," *Massachusetts Review* 12 (Winter 1971): 48. See also Joyce Piell Wexler, *Laura Riding's Pursuit of Truth* (Athens, Ohio: Ohio University Press, 1979), 139–52.
9. Herbert Marcuse, *An Essay on Liberation* (Boston: Beacon Press, 1969), 40–41.
10. The experience of Czeslaw Miłosz, according to Ted Hughes, Introduction to *Collected Poems of Vasko Popa, 1943–1976*, trans. Anne Pennington (Manchester: Carcanet Press, 1978), 1–2.
11. Ted Hughes in an interview with Tom Stoppard, *Times Literary Supplement*, 1 October 1971, quoted in A. C. H. Smith, *Orghast at Persepolis* (New York: Viking, 1972), 3.
12. Letter to Richard Woodhouse, October 1818 in *The Letters of John Keats*, ed. Hyder Rollins (Cambridge, Mass.: Harvard, 1958), 1:387.
13. M. L. Rosenthal, "Modern British and American Poetic Sequences," *Contemporary Literature* 18 (Summer 1977): 417–18.
14. David Jones, Preface, *The Anathémata*, 33.

Notes

15. Charles Altieri, "Presence and Reference in a Literary Text: The Example of Williams' 'This is Just to Say,'" *Critical Inquiry* 5 (Spring 1979): 492.

16. Roy Fisher, *Nineteen Poems and an Interview*, 23.

17. James D. Watson, *The Double Helix* (New York: New American Library, 1968), 131.

18. Note on dust jacket of *Landscapes*.

19. Quoted in R. L. Feigen, ed., *Claude Monet* (New York: Feigen and Co., 1969), 11.

20. Quoted in Herbert Read, *The Philosophy of Modern Art* (London: Faber & Faber, 1954), 23–24.

21. John Cage, *Silence* (Middletown, Conn.: Wesleyan University Press, 1961), 95.

22. Quoted in Marjorie G. Perloff, "New Thresholds, Old Anatomies: Contemporary Poetry and the Limits of Exegesis," *Iowa Review* 5 (Winter 1974): 89.

Notes to Chapter 2:
Charles Tomlinson

1. Wilhelm Worringer, *Abstraction and Empathy*, trans. Michael Bullock (London: Routledge & Kegan Paul, 1963), 15–16, 44.

2. "Dates: Penkhull New Road," *The Way In*.

3. The relationship is the subject of "Class," ibid.

4. Charles Tomlinson, in Ian Hamilton, "Four Conversations," *London Magazine*, n.s., 4 (November 1964): 82–83.

5. "Prometheus," *The Way of a World*.

6. "Elegy for Henry Street," *Written on Water*.

7. *A Peopled Landscape*.

8. "Over Brooklyn Bridge," ibid.

9. "During Rain," *Written on Water*.

10. "Before the Dance," *The Way of a World*.

11. "The Poet as a Painter," *Christian Science Monitor*, 7 March 1974.

12. *Written on Water*.

13. Both graphics are reproduced in Tomlinson's *Words and Images*.

14. "Eden," *The Way of a World*.

15. "Rhymes," *The Shaft*.

16. *Seeing is Believing*.

17. Lucy R. Lippard, Introduction to *Pop Art* (London: Thames and Hudson, 1966), 18; Edward Lucie-Smith, Introduction to *British Painting and Sculpture 1960–1970* (London: Tate Gallery Publications, 1970), 44.

18. "Unregarded Congruence," *Times Literary Supplement*, 9 August 1963, 610.

19. In a letter to the author, 6 October 1977.

Notes

20. Charles Tomlinson, *The Poem as Initiation* (Hamilton, N.Y.: Colgate University Press, 1968). Quoted by Richard Ellmann and Robert O'Clair, eds., in *The Norton Anthology of Modern Poetry* (New York: W. W. Norton, 1973), 1152. They consider the remark, specifically related to "Swimming Chenango Lake," to be "relevant to much of his other work."
21. "Composition," *The Way of a World*.
22. *The Way In*.
23. "Not in Sequence of a Metronome," *Agenda* 10–11 (Autumn–Winter 1972–1973): 54.
24. *American Scenes*.
25. "The Poet as a Painter."
26. "A Self-Portrait: David," *The Shaft*.
27. "Skullshapes," *The Way of a World*.
28. "Mistlines," *Written on Water*.
29. "Night Transfigured," *The Way of a World*.
30. *The Necklace*.
31. *A Peopled Landscape*.
32. *Written on Water*.
33. *The Way of a World*.
34. *The Shaft*.
35. Rosemarie Waldrop, "Charles Olson: Process and Relationship," *Twentieth Century Literature* 23 (December 1977): 469.
36. "Against Portraits," *Written on Water*.
37. Preface to *The Necklace*.
38. In "Not in Sequence of a Metronome," 53.
39. *The Way of a World*.
40. "Appearance," *Written on Water*.
41. "Drive," *Written on Water*.
42. "Le Musée Imaginaire," *A Peopled Landscape*.
43. *The Way of a World*.
44. *The Necklace*.
45. *The Way of a World*.
46. *A Peopled Landscape*.
47. *The Way of a World*.
48. "Logic," ibid.

Notes to Chapter 3:
Roy Fisher

1. "The Poplars," in *City, Collected Poems 1968*. Except where noted, references to *City* are from this volume.
2. *Nineteen Poems and an Interview*, 15.
3. Ibid., 23.
4. *The Cut Pages*, 6.

Notes

5. *City.*

6. "The Intruder," *Collected Poems 1968.*

7. *City.*

8. *Nineteen Poems and an Interview,* 34.

9. Roy Fisher, in Eric Mottram, "Conversation with Roy Fisher," *Saturday Morning* 1 (Spring 1976).

10. Donald Davie, *Thomas Hardy and British Poetry* (New York: Oxford University Press, 1972), 171.

11. *Nineteen Poems and an Interview,* 18.

12. Robin Fulton, review of *Collected Poems 1968,* in *Stand* 11 (1969–1970): 70.

13. *City,* 3.

14. *The Ship's Orchestra,* 11–12.

15. *Collected Poems,* 37–38.

16. Nine of the poems are reprinted in *Collected Poems* as "Interiors with Various Figures."

17. *Nineteen Poems and an Interview,* 13.

18. Ibid., 14.

19. *The Ship's Orchestra,* 22.

20. Ibid., 29–30.

21. Ibid., 41.

22. Ibid., 36.

23. Ibid., 25.

24. Ibid., 21–22.

25. Ibid., 15.

26. "I talk about ordinary people who die and their death is given ceremony on an almost Yeatsian level. But they're certainly portrayed as dead who have been tricked and bamboozled by the world itself. As if the principles of the world are illusory, that people are dupes of creation." Fisher, *Nineteen Poems and an Interview,* 23.

27. Mottram, "Conversation with Roy Fisher."

28. "Glenthorne Poems," no. 7.

29. Davie, *Thomas Hardy and British Poetry,* 169. "Toyland" now appears in *Collected Poems.*

30. *Times Literary Supplement,* 24 January 1969, 828.

31. Victor Shklovsky, *Sur La Theorie de la Prose,* trans. Guy Verret (1929; reprint, Lausanne: Editions l'Age d'homme, 1973), quoted in Robert Scholes, *Structuralism in Literature* (New Haven: Yale University Press, 1974), 63.

32. Author's note, *The Cut Pages,* 7.

33. Ibid., 6–7.

34. J. H. Needham, "Some Aspects of the Poetry of Roy Fisher," *Poetry Nation* 5 (1975): 86.

Notes

Notes to Chapter 4:
Matthew Mead

1. *Identities and Other Poems.*
2. *Contemporary Poets of the English Language*, ed. Rosalie Murphy (London: St. James Press, 1970), 742.
3. Christopher Middleton, quoted in Ian Hamilton, "Four Conversations," *London Magazine*, n.s., 4 (November 1964): 80.
4. *Contemporary Poets of the English Language*, 742.
5. Heinz Winfried Sabais, "Dream," *Generation and Other Poems*, trans. Ruth and Matthew Mead (Northwood, Middlesex: Anvil Press, 1968), 11. All references to Sabais's poetry are from this volume.
6. *Identities.*
7. *Minusland*, 9–13.
8. *Identities.*
9. I. M. L. Hunter, *Memory* (Harmondsworth, Middlesex: Penguin, 1957), 57.

Notes to Chapter 5:
Geoffrey Hill

1. Radcliffe Squires, *Allen Tate: A Literary Biography* (New York: Pegasus, 1971), 213.
2. *Somewhere Is Such a Kingdom.*
3. On the double meanings in the opening stanza of this poem, see Christopher Ricks, "Cliché as 'Responsible Speech'; Geoffrey Hill," *London Magazine* 4 (November 1964): 96–101.
4. *Somewhere Is Such a Kingdom*, 125.
5. Ibid.
6. In the notes to *King Log*, Hill reprints the poem, somewhat revised, and says, "I dislike the poem very much and the publication of this amended version may be regarded as a necessary penitential exercise."
7. *Somewhere Is Such a Kingdom.*
8. Ibid.
9. Harold Bloom, "Introduction: The Survival of Strong Poetry," *Somewhere Is Such a Kingdom*, xxiv.
10. John Frederick Nims, ed. and trans., "Considerations," *The Poems of St. John of the Cross*, 3d ed. (Chicago: University of Chicago Press, 1979), 128.
11. Ibid., 120.
12. Merle E. Brown, *Double Lyric* (New York: Columbia, 1980), 67.
13. Ibid., 70–71, Brown quoting the theologian D. M. MacKinnon.

Notes

Notes to Chapter 6:
Ted Hughes

1. Ekbert Faas, "Ted Hughes and Crow," *London Magazine*, n.s., 10 (January 1971): 20.

2. Hughes: "[Vasko] Popa, and several other writers one can think of, have in a way cut their losses and cut the whole hopelessness of that civilization off, have somehow managed to invest their hopes in something deeper than what you lose if civilization disappears completely and in a way it's obviously a pervasive and deep feeling that civilization has now disappeared completely. If it's still here it's still here by grace of pure inertia and chance and if the whole thing has essentially vanished one had better have one's spirit invested in something that will not vanish. And this is a shifting of your foundation to completely new Holy Ground, a new divinity, one that won't be under the rubble when the churches collapse." Ibid., 19.

3. Quoted in A. C. H. Smith, *Orghast at Persepolis* (New York: Viking, 1972), 244.

4. Performed in Iran. See ibid.

5. "Thrushes."

6. "Bullfrog."

7. "Hawk Roosting."

8. Faas, "Ted Hughes and Crow," 8.

9. Ibid., 10–11.

10. George Steiner, *Language and Silence* (New York: Atheneum, 1967), ix.

11. Introduction to Vasko Popa, *Collected Poems 1943–1976*, trans. Anne Pennington (Manchester: Carcanet, 1978), 1–2. All quotations of Popa's poetry are from this edition.

12. John Bayley, "Smash and Bash," *The Listener*, 2 June 1977, 726.

13. Ted Hughes, "Secret Ecstasie," *The Listener*, 29 October 1964, 677.

14. Daniel Hoffman, "Talking Beasts: The 'Single Adventure' in the Poems of Ted Hughes," *Shenandoah* 19 (Summer 1968): 63–64.

15. *Wodwo*, 45.

16. Ibid., 55.

17. Ibid., 69.

18. Ibid., 91.

19. Ibid., 109, 144.

20. Keith Sagar, *The Art of Ted Hughes* (Cambridge: The University Press, 1975), 61.

21. Faas, "Ted Hughes and Crow," 11.

22. Sagar, *The Art of Ted Hughes*, 107.

23. Ted Hughes, "Words and Experience," *Poetry in the Making* (London: Faber, 1967), 120. Quoted in Sagar.

Notes

24. Henri Chopin, "Why I Am the Author of Sound Poetry and Free Poetry," trans. Irene Montjoye Sinor and Mary Ellen Solt, 1967; quoted in Mary Ellen Solt, ed., *Concrete Poetry: A World View* (Bloomington: Indiana University Press, 1970), 71.

25. C. V. Fernandez, "*Crow*: A Mythology of the Demonic," *Modern Poetry Studies* 6 (Autumn 1975): 144–56.

26. Sagar, *The Art of Ted Hughes*, 115.

27. Faas, "Ted Hughes and Crow," 10.

28. Ibid., 19.

29. John Crowe Ransom, "Thomas Hardy's Poems and the Religious Difficulties of a Naturalist," *Kenyon Review* 22 (Spring 1960): 193.

30. David Lodge, "*Crow* and the Cartoons," *Critical Quarterly* 13 (Spring 1971): 37–42.

31. "A Disaster."

32. "That Moment."

33. "Crow's Song of Himself."

34. Introduction to Vasko Popa, *Collected Poems*, 10.

35. Peter Dale, "Ted Hughes's *Crow*," *Agenda* 9 (Spring–Summer 1971): 99.

36. "The whole myth was to be told as an epic folk-tale in prose with songs by and about Crow interspersed. A good deal of unpublished material exists, but it is unlikely that the project will ever be completed. Very few of the poems in *Crow* demand a knowledge of the mythic framework, a good deal of which can, in any case, be deduced from the poems themselves." Sagar also quotes Hughes's account of *Crow* on the Claddagh record, noting that "it describes largely a part of the Crow story Hughes never reached in the poems." Sagar, *The Art of Ted Hughes*, 106, 118.

37. Herbert Marcuse, *An Essay on Liberation* (Boston: Beacon Press, 1969), 44.

38. Leo Steinberg, "Contemporary Art and the Plight of Its Public," in *The New Art*, ed. Gregory Battcock (New York: Dutton, 1966), 43.

39. Faas, "Ted Hughes and Crow," 18.

40. "Context," *London Magazine*, n.s., 1 (February 1962): 45.

41. Quoted in Smith, *Orghast at Persepolis*, 44–45.

42. Susan Sontag, *Styles of Radical Will* (New York: Delta, 1970), 12.

43. Hughes, "Words and Experience," 119–20.

44. *Gaudete*, 166.

45. Ibid., 23.

46. Ibid., 128.

47. Bayley, "Smash and Bash," 726.

48. Edwin Morgan, "Gods of Mud," *The Listener*, 7 September 1978, 318.

49. Sagar, *The Art of Ted Hughes*, 157.

50. Peter Porter, "Poetry," *The Observer* (London), 27 January 1980, 39.

Notes

51. Terry Eagleton, "Recent Poetry," *Stand* 21 (1980): 80.

52. Peter Scupham, "The Demon-farmer's Carnival," *Times Literary Supplement*, 4 January 1980, 6.

Notes to Chapter 7:
David Jones

1. Samuel Reese, *David Jones* (Boston: Twayne, 1978), 75.

2. *In Parenthesis* (1963), 77.

3. Ibid., xi.

4. M. Mott, "Recent Developments in British Poetry," *Poetry* 118 (May 1971): 103.

5. Monroe Spears, "Shapes and Surfaces: David Jones, with a Glance at Charles Tomlinson," *Contemporary Literature* 12 (Autumn 1971): 410.

6. Quoted in John H. Johnston, *English Poetry of the First World War* (Princeton: Princeton University Press, 1964), 322. Johnston discusses the influence of *The Waste Land* at some length.

7. Jeremy Hooker, "Brut's Albion," in *David Jones: Eight Essays on His Work*, ed. Roland Mathias (Wales: Gomer Press, 1976), 123–24.

8. Howard Nemerov, "Seven Poets and the Language," *Sewanee Review* 62 (Spring 1954): 314.

9. *Anathémata* (1963), 106n.

10. Ibid., 53.

11. Ibid., 84.

12. Reese, *David Jones*, 82.

13. *Anathémata*, 180–81.

14. Ibid., 200n.

15. *The Sleeping Lord and Other Fragments*, 70.

16. *Anathémata*, 89.

17. David Jones, "Past and Present," *Epoch and Artist*, 141.

18. *Anathémata*, 82n.

19. Ibid., 68.

20. Quoted in David Blamires, *David Jones: Artist and Writer* (Manchester: Manchester University Press, 1971), 59.

21. David Jones, *Letters to Vernon Watkins*, ed. Ruth Pryor, 78.

22. Douglas Cleverdon, *Word and Image*, no. 12 (National Book League Exhibition Catalog, 1972), 8.

23. *The Sleeping Lord.*

24. *Anathémata*, 121.

25. David Jones, "The Eclipse of a Hymn," *Epoch and Artist*, 261.

26. *The Sleeping Lord.*

27. *Anathémata*, 239.

28. Ibid., 20.

29. Ibid., 200.

30. Ibid., 84.

31. According to John Heath-Stubbs, reviewing David Blamires's *Da-*

Notes

vid Jones: Artist and Writer, in *Agenda* 9–10 (Autumn–Winter 1971–1972): 94.

32. Spears, "Shapes and Surfaces," 406.

33. John Heath–Stubbs's review of *The Tribune's Visitation*, *Poetry Review* (Summer 1970): 168.

34. Jones, preface to *Anathémata*, 33.

35. Ibid., 31–32.

36. Ibid., 29.

37. Jones, "A Note on Mr. Berenson's Views," *Epoch and Artist*, 277.

38. Jones, "If and Perhaps and But," *Epoch and Artist*, 278.

39. *The Tribune's Visitation* (no page numbers).

40. Blamires, *David Jones: Artist and Writer*, 115.

41. *Anathémata*, 34.

42. Blamires, *David Jones: Artist and Writer*, 119. This passage is quoted by Blamires from Gwyn Williams's foreword to *The Burning Tree*, ed. Gwyn Williams (London: Faber and Faber, 1956), 15.

43. Jones, "Autobiographical Talk," *Epoch and Artist*, 31.

44. Kenneth Clark, "Some Recent Paintings of David Jones," *Agenda* 5 (Spring–Summer 1967): 100.

Notes to Chapter 8:
Basil Bunting

1. "Muzzle and jowl and beastly brow," *Collected Poems*. All quotations of Bunting's poetry come from this volume.

2. "As appleblossom to crocus."

3. "See! Their verses are laid."

4. Note to *Briggflatts*, ibid., 148.

5. Hugh Kenner, "Never a Boast or a See-Here," *National Review*, 31 October 1967, 1217.

6. "The day being Whitsun we had pigeon for dinner."

7. Anthony Suter, "Time and the Literary Past in the Poetry of Basil Bunting," *Contemporary Literature* 12 (Autumn 1971): 525.

8. Charles Tomlinson, "Experience into Music: The Poetry of Basil Bunting," *Agenda* 4 (Autumn 1966): 15.

9. Richard Ellmann and Robert O'Clair, eds., *The Norton Anthology of Modern Poetry* (New York: W. W. Norton, 1973), 615.

10. "Basil Bunting: A Letter," *Agenda* 10–11 (Autumn–Winter 1972–1973): 12.

11. Reminiscent of the report that he once joined a hostile crowd outside his house in Persia, chanting, "Death to Mr. Bunting."

12. Quoted by R. S. Woolf, "Basil Bunting's Poetry," *Stand* 8 (1966): 28.

13. Alain Robbe-Grillet, *Last Year at Marienbad*, trans. Richard Howard (New York: Grove, 1962), 14.

14. Anthony Suter, "Art and Experience: An Approach to Basil Bunt-

ing's Ideal of Poetry and the Poet," *Durham University Journal* 66 (June 1974): 35.

15. Anthony Suter, "Basil Bunting, Poet of the Modern Times," *Ariel* 3, no. 4 (1972): 28.

16. *Collected Poems*, 45.

17. Kenneth Cox, "The Aesthetic of Basil Bunting," *Agenda* 4 (Autumn 1966): 24.

Notes to Chapter 9:
Anselm Hollo

1. "the day's events," *Sojourner Microcosms*.
2. "los sedentarios," ibid.
3. "out of this world," ibid.
4. *Alembic*, 55.
5. *Faces and Forms*.
6. "the empress hotel poems."
7. "the day's events," *Sojourner Microcosms*.
8. *& it is a song*.
9. "Shu," *Sojourner Microcosms*.
10. "Write the Poem," *Kulchur* 3 (Autumn 1963): 71.
11. "hot moon, & still looking," *Alembic*.
12. *Sojourner Microcosms*.
13. *Alembic*.
14. "the monster," *Sojourner Microcosms*.
15. *Faces and Forms*.
16. "the i.s.s.," *Maya*.
17. *Contemporary Poets of the English Language*, ed. Rosalie Murphy (Chicago: St. James Press, 1970), 519.
18. *Sojourner Microcosms*.
19. Ibid.
20. Ibid.
21. "song of the tusk," ibid.
22. Ibid.
23. "the trees at 2 a.m.," *Maya*.
24. *Sojourner Microcosms*.
25. Ibid.
26. *Faces and Forms*.
27. *Sojourner Microcosms*.
28. *Maya*.
29. *& it is a song*.
30. "The World Outside," *Faces and Forms*.
31. *Sojourner Microcosms*.

Notes

32. "the day's events," ibid.
33. *& it is a song.*

Notes to Chapter 10:
Lee Harwood

1. Hayden Carruth, in *Contemporary Poets of the English Language*, ed. Rosalie Murphy (Chicago: St. James Press, 1970), 614.
2. "The American Action Painters," *The Tradition of the New* (New York: Horizon, 1959), 25.
3. James Schuyler, in *The New American Poetry, 1945–1960*, ed. Donald M. Allen (New York: Grove Press, 1960), 418.
4. *HMS Little Fox*, 11.
5. Lee Harwood, "A Conversation" with Eric Mottram, *Poetry Information*, no. 14 (Autumn–Winter 1975–1976): 10.
6. "When the Geography Was Fixed" and "In Bed."
7. *The White Room.*
8. *HMS Little Fox*, 75–92.
9. Ibid., 13.
10. *The White Room.*
11. "The Book," ibid.
12. *Old Bosham Bird Watch and Other Stories*, no page numbers.
13. *The White Room.*
14. Ibid.
15. "The Blue Mosque," ibid.
16. "The Ache?," *The Sinking Colony.*
17. Harwood, "A Conversation" with Eric Mottram, 13.
18. *Landscapes.*
19. Ibid.
20. *Old Bosham Bird Watch and Other Stories.*
21. *The White Room.*
22. Ibid.
23. "The Words," *The Sinking Colony.*
24. Note on dust jacket of *Landscapes.*
25. *Landscapes.*
26. "Plato Was Right Though," *The White Room.*
27. "The 'Utopia.'"
28. Harwood's note on dust jacket.
29. Harwood, "A Conversation" with Eric Mottram, 12.

Notes

Notes to Chapter 11:
Tom Raworth

1. Quoted in Edward Lucie-Smith, "Pop Art," *Concepts of Modern Art,* ed. Tony Richardson and Nikos Stangos (Harmondsworth, Middlesex: Penguin, 1974), 226.

2. Morse Peckham, *Man's Rage for Chaos* (New York: Chilton, 1965), xi, 33, 314.

3. Tom Raworth, interview with Barry Alpert, *Vort,* no. 1 (Fall 1972): 43.

4. Ibid., 41–42.

5. Charles Olson, "Projective Verse," *Human Universe and Other Essays,* ed. Donald Allen (New York: Grove, 1967), 56.

6. Gael Turnbull, "Resonances and Speculations: Upon Reading Roy Fisher's *City,*" *Kulchur* 2 (Autumn 1962): 27. Quoted in *Children of Albion,* ed. Michael Horowitz (Harmondsworth, Middlesex: Penguin, 1969), 319.

7. Raworth, interview with Alpert, 41.

8. H. Williams, "Poetry: Strolling Across the Bridge," review of *Lion, Lion,* in *London Magazine,* February 1971, 78.

9. "These Are Not Catastrophes I Went Out of My Way to Look For," *The Big Green Day.*

10. Review of *Moving, Times Literary Supplement,* 16 April 1971, 439.

11. Victor Shklovsky, *Sur La Theorie de la Prose,* trans. Guy Verret (1929; reprint ed., Lausanne: Éditions l'Age d'homme, 1973), quoted in Robert Scholes, *Structuralism in Literature* (New Haven: Yale University Press, 1974), 83.

12. *The Relation Ship.*

13. *Big Green Day,* 16.

14. "Love Poem," ibid.

15. "All His Days & All Her Days Making His Breakfast," ibid.

16. "The Blown Agent," ibid.

17. "Bitter Moon Dances," *The Relation Ship.*

18. "Wedding Day," ibid.

19. *Moving.*

20. Raworth, interview with Alpert, 34.

21. Ibid.

22. Ibid., 44.

23. Ibid., 45.

24. Both poems are from *Big Green Day.*

25. "The Lonely Life of the Lighthouse Keeper," ibid.

26. Ibid.

27. Edward Lucie-Smith, *Movements in Art Since 1945* (London: Thames and Hudson, 1969), 123–24.

Notes

28. John Cage, "Experimental Music," in *Silence* (London: Calder and Boyers, 1968), 8.
29. *Back to Nature*, to which the whole issue of *Joe DiMaggio*, no. 4 (1973), is devoted.
30. Roland Barthes, *Writing Degree Zero*, trans. Annette Lavers and Colin Smith (Cape Editions 3, London: Jonathan Cape, 1967), 47.
31. *Fix*, no. 1 (May 1974), no page numbers.
32. Ibid.
33. "Tracking (notes)," *Act*.

Notes to Chapter 12:
Conclusion

1. Frank Kermode, *The Sense of an Ending* (New York: Oxford University Press, 1968), 129.
2. Allan Kaprow, *Assemblage, Environments and Happenings* (New York: Harvey N. Abrams, 1966), 156.
3. *Ancient Art and Ritual*, quoted by Stephen Spender, "Notebook V," *London Magazine*, June–July 1975, 31.
4. D. H. Lawrence, "Poetry of the Present," introduction to the American edition of *New Poems 1918*, in *The Complete Poems of D. H. Lawrence*, ed. Vivian de Sola Pinto and F. Warren Roberts (New York: Viking, 1971), 184.

Bibliography of Works by the Poets

Charles Tomlinson

Relations and Contraries. Aldington, Kent: The Hand and Flower Press, 1951.

The Necklace. Eynsham, Oxfordshire: Fantasy Press, 1955; revised, London and New York: University Press, 1966.

Solo For a Glass Harmonica. San Francisco: Westerham Press, 1957 (poems in folio).

Seeing Is Believing. New York: McDowell, Obolensky, 1958; London: Oxford University Press, 1960.

A Peopled Landscape: Poems. London and New York: Oxford University Press, 1963.

Poems: A Selection (with Tony Connor and Austin Clarke). London: Oxford University Press, 1964.

American Scenes and Other Poems. London and New York: Oxford University Press, 1966.

The Poem As Initiation. Hamilton, N.Y.: Colgate University Press, 1968.

The Mattachines: New Mexico. Cerillos, N. Mex.: San Marcos Press, 1968.

To Be Engraved On the Skull Of a Cormorant. Serpent Papers, no. 1. London: The Unaccompanied Serpent, 1968.

The Way of a World. London and New York: Oxford University Press, 1969.

American West Southwest. Cerillos, N. Mex.: San Marcos Press, 1969.

A New Kind Of Tie. Nottingham: Tarasque Press, 1972.

Words and Images. London: Covent Garden Press, 1972.

Written On Water. London: Oxford University Press, 1972.

The Way of a World. London and New York: Oxford University Press, 1969.

American West Southwest. Cerillos, N. Mex.: San Marcos Press, 1969.

Selected Poems 1951–1974. Oxford and New York: Oxford University Press, 1978.

The Flood. Oxford and New York: Oxford University Press, 1981.

Roy Fisher

City. Worcester, England: Migrant Press, 1961.

Then Hallucinations: City II. Worcester, England: Migrant Press, 1961.

Bibliography

The Ship's Orchestra. London: Fulcrum Press, 1966.
Ten Interiors With Various Figures. Trent Bridge, Nottingham: Tarasque Press, 1967.
The Memorial Fountain. Newcastle upon Tyne: Northern House, 1967.
Titles. Trent Bridge, Nottingham: Tarasque Press, 1969.
Collected Poems 1968. London: Fulcrum Press, 1969.
Correspondence (with Tom Phillips). London: Tetrad Press, 1970.
Metamorphoses. London: Tetrad Press, 1970.
Matrix. London: Fulcrum Press, 1971.
The Cut Pages. London: Fulcrum Press, 1971. Includes *Metamorphoses* and other poetry.
Also There. London: Tetrad Press, 1972.
Bluebeard's Castle. Guildford, Surrey: Circle Press Publications, 1972.
Cultures. London: Tetrad Press, 1975.
Nineteen Poems and an Interview. Pensnett, Staffordshire: Grossteste, 1975.
Neighbours We'll Not Part Tonight! Guildford, Surrey: For the Demon Knitters of Dent. Circle Press Publications, 1976.
Four Poems. Newcastle upon Tyne: Pig Press, 1976.
Barnardine's Reply. Knotting, Bedfordshire: Sceptre Press, 1977.
Scenes From the Alphabet. Guildford, Surrey: Circle Press Publications, 1978.
The Thing About Joe Sullivan: Poems, 1971–1977. Manchester: Carcanet New Press, 1978.
Comedies. Newcastle upon Tyne: Pig Press, 1979; reprinted as *Consolidated Comedies.*
Poems 1955–80. Oxford and New York: Oxford University Press, 1980. Includes *The Ship's Orchestra, Collected Poems 1968, The Thing About Joe Sullivan,* selections from *The Cut Pages,* and other poetry.

Matthew Mead

A Poem in Nine Parts. Worcester, England, and Ventura, Calif.: Migrant Press, 1960.
Identities. Worcester, England: Migrant Press, 1964; London: Rapp & Carroll, 1967.
Kleinigkeiten. Newcastle upon Tyne: Malcolm Rutherford for *Satis,* 1966.
Identities and Other Poems. London: Rapp & Carroll, 1967.
The Administration of Things. London: Anvil Press Poetry, 1970.
In the Eyes of the People. Edinburgh: Malcolm Rutherford for *Satis,* 1973.
Minusland. Edinburgh: Malcolm Rutherford for *Satis,* 1977.
Midday Muse. London: Anvil Press Poetry, 1979.

Bibliography

Geoffrey Hill

Poems. Fantasy Poets Series, no. 11. Oxford: Oxford University Poetry Society, 1953.
For the Unfallen: Poems 1952–1958. London: Andre Deutsch, 1959; Chester Springs, Pa.: Dufour Editions, 1960.
Preghiere (with Edwin Brock and Stevie Smith). Leeds: School of English, Leeds University, 1964.
King Log. London: Andre Deutsch, 1968; Chester Springs, Pa.: Dufour Editions, 1968.
Mercian Hymns. London: Andre Deutsch, 1971.
Somewhere Is Such a Kingdom: Poems 1952–1971. Boston: Houghton Mifflin, 1975. Contains *For the Unfallen, King Log,* and *Mercian Hymns.*
Tenebrae. London: Andre Deutsch, 1978; Boston: Houghton Mifflin, 1979.

Ted Hughes

Volumes are chronologically ordered except where Crow material has been grouped. For the location of poems appearing only in periodicals and a more complete description of the contents of books and pamphlets, including differences between British and American editions, see the bibliographies appended to Keith Sagar's *The Art of Ted Hughes,* 2d ed. (Cambridge and New York: Cambridge University Press, 1978) and Terry Gifford and Neil Roberts's *Ted Hughes: A Critical Study* (London and Boston: Faber and Faber, 1981).

The Hawk in the Rain. London: Faber and Faber, 1957; New York: Harper & Brothers, 1957.
Lupercal. London: Faber and Faber, 1960; New York: Harper & Brothers, 1960.
Selected Poems (with Thom Gunn). London: Faber and Faber, 1962.
The Earth-Owl and Other Moon-People. London: Faber and Faber, 1963.
The Burning of the Brothel. London: Turret Books, 1966.
Recklings. London: Turret Books, 1966.
Scapegoats and Rabies: a Poem In Five Parts. London: Poet and Printer, 1967.
Animal Poems. Crediton, Devonshire: Richard Gilbertson, 1967.
Wodwo. London: Faber and Faber, 1967; New York: Harper & Row Publishers, 1967.
Five Autumn Songs For Children's Voices. Crediton, Devonshire: Richard Gilbertson, 1967.
The Martyrdom of Bishop Farrar. Crediton, Devonshire: Richard Gilbertson, 1970.

Crow: From the Life and Songs of the Crow. London: Faber and Faber, 1970;

revised, New York: Harper & Row, 1971; London: Faber and Faber, 1972; 1973; 1974.

A Few Crows. Exeter: Rougemont Press, 1970.

A Crow Hymn. Farnham, Surrey: Sceptre Press, 1970.

Crow Wakes. Woodford Green, Essex: Poet and Printer, 1971.

Eat Crow. London: Rainbow Press, 1971.

Shakespeare's Poem. London: Lexham Press, 1971.

Poems (with Ruth Fainlight and Alan Sillitoe). London: Rainbow Press, 1971.

In the Little Girl's Gaze. London: Steam Press, 1972.

Selected Poems 1957–1967. London: Faber and Faber, 1972; New York: Harper & Row, 1973.

Prometheus on His Crag: 21 Poems. London: Rainbow Press, 1973.

Spring, Summer, Autumn, Winter. London: Rainbow Press, 1974.

Season Songs. New York: Viking Press, 1975; London: Faber and Faber, 1976.

Cave Birds. London: Scolar Press, 1975. Revised as *Cave Birds: An Alchemical Cave Drama.* London: Faber and Faber, 1978; New York: Viking Press, 1978.

Moon-Whales and Other Poems. New York: Viking Press, 1976. Includes *The Earth-Moon* and most of *Earth-Owl.*

Eclipse. Knotting, Bedfordshire: Sceptre Press, 1976.

Earth-Moon. London: Rainbow Press, 1976.

Gaudete. London: Faber and Faber, 1977; New York: Harper & Row, 1977; London: Faber and Faber, 1979.

Sunstruck. Knotting, Bedfordshire: Sceptre Press, 1977.

Chiasmadon. Baltimore: Charles Seluzicki, 1977.

Moortown Elegies. London: Rainbow Press, 1978.

Moon-Bells and Other Poems. London: Chatto and Windus, 1978.

A Solstice. Knotting, Bedfordshire: Sceptre Press, 1978.

Calder Valley Poems. London: Rainbow Press, 1978.

Orts. London: Rainbow Press, 1978.

Adam and the Sacred Nine. London: Rainbow Press, 1979.

Moortown. London: Faber and Faber, 1979; New York: Harper & Row, 1979. Includes selections from *Cave Birds, Prometheus on His Crag, Orts, Adam and the Sacred Nine,* and other poetry.

Remains of Elmet: A Pennine Sequence. London: Rainbow Press, 1979; London: Faber and Faber, 1979; New York: Harper & Row, 1979.

All Around the Year (with Michael Morpurgo). London: John Murray Publishers, 1979.

Brooktrout. North Tawton, Devonshire: Morrigu Press, 1979.

Four Tales Told by an Idiot. Knotting, Bedfordshire: Sceptre Press, 1979.

Wolverine. North Tawton, Devonshire: Morrigu Press, 1979.

Under the North Star. New York: Viking Press, 1981; London: Faber and Faber, 1981.

New Selected Poems. New York: Harper & Row, 1982; London: Faber and Faber, 1982.

David Jones

In Parenthesis: Seinnyessit E Gledyf YM Penn Mameu. London: Faber and Faber, 1937; New York: Chilmark Press, 1962.
The Anathémata: Fragments of an Attempted Writing. London: Faber and Faber, 1952; New York: Chilmark Press, 1963.
Epoch and Artist. London: Faber and Faber, 1959.
The Fatigue. Cambridge: Rampant Lions Press, 1965.
The Tribune's Visitation. London: Fulcrum Press, 1969.
The Sleeping Lord, and Other Fragments. London: Faber and Faber, 1974. Includes *The Fatigue, The Tribune's Visitation,* and other poetry.
The Kensington Mass. London: Agenda Editions, 1975.
Letters to Vernon Watkins. Edited by Ruth Pryor. Cardiff: University of Wales Press, 1976.

Basil Bunting

Redimiculum Matellarum. Milan: Grafica Moderna, 1930.
Poems 1950. Galveston, Tex.: Cleaners' Press, 1950.
First Books of Odes. London: Fulcrum Press, 1965.
Loquitur. London: Fulcrum Press, 1965. Selections from *Poems 1950, First Books of Odes,* and other previously published poetry.
The Spoils. Newcastle upon Tyne: Morden Tower Book Room, 1965.
Ode II/2. London: Fulcrum Press, 1965.
Briggflatts. London: Fulcrum Press, 1966.
Two Poems. Santa Barbara, Calif.: Unicorn Press, 1967.
What the Chairman Told Tom. Cambridge, Mass.: Pym-Randall Press, 1967.
Collected Poems. London: Fulcrum Press, 1968; revised, Oxford and New York: Oxford University Press, 1978.
Version of Horace. London: Holborn Publishing, 1972.

Anselm Hollo

Lover Man. New York: The dead language press, 1961.
St Texts & Finnpoems. Worcester, England: Migrant Press, 1961.
Poems: We Just Wanted To Tell You (with David Bell). Lichfield Grove, England: Writers Forum, 1961.
& What Else Is New, a Small Pamphlet. Kent: New Voice, 1963.

Bibliography

History. London: Matrix Press, 1963.
& It Is a Song: Poems. Birmingham: Migrant Press, 1965.
Faces & Forms. London: Ambit Books, 1965.
Here We Go. The Stranger's Press, 1965.
The Claim. London: Goliard Press, 1965.
The Going-On Poem. London: Writers Forum, 1966.
Isadora, And Other Poems. London: Writers Forum, 1967.
Leaf Times. Exeter: University of Exeter, 1967.
Buffalo–Isle of Wight Power Cable. Buffalo: Department of English, State
    University of New York at Buffalo, 1967.
The Man in the Treetop Hat. London: Turret Books, 1968.
The Coherences. London: Trigram Press, 1968.
Haiku (with John Esam and Tom Raworth). London: Trigram Press,
    1968.
Tumbleweed: Poems. Toronto: Weed/flower Press, 1968.
Waiting For a Beautiful Bather: Ten Poems. Milwaukee: Morgan Press,
    1969.
Doubletalk (with Ted Berrigan; set by T. G. Miller). Iowa City: Nomad
    Press, 1969.
Maya: Works 1959–1969. London: Cape Goliard, 1970; New York: Gross-
    man Publishers, 1970.
Gee Apollinaire: Birth of a Poem, a Documentary Poem. Iowa City: Nomad
    Press, 1970.
Message. Santa Barbara, Calif.: Unicorn Press, 1970.
Alembic. London: Trigram Press, 1972.
America del Norte & Other Peace Herb Poems. Toronto: Weed/flower Press,
    1970.
Sensation 27. Canton, N.Y.: The Institute of Further Studies, 1972.
Spring Cleaning Greens, From Notebooks 1967–1973. Bowling Green, Ohio:
    Doones Press, 1973.
Smoke Writing. Storrs, Conn.: University of Connecticut Library, 1973.
Black Book. Bowling Green, Ohio: Black Book Press, 1974.
Anselm Hollo. Center Conway, N.H.: Walker's Pond Press, 1974.
Some Worlds. New Rochelle, N.Y.: The Elizabeth Press, 1974.
Mano. Okemos, Mich.: Stone Press, 1975.
Heavy Jars. West Branch, Iowa: Toothpaste Press, 1977.
Lingering Tangos. Baltimore: Tropos Press, 1977.
Sojourner Microcosms: New & Selected Poems 1959–1977. Berkeley: Blue
    Wind Press, 1977.
Curious Data. Buffalo: White Pine, 1978.
Lunch in Fur. St. Paul: Truck Press, 1978.
With Ruth In Mind. Barryton, N.Y.: Station Hill Press, 1979.
Finite Continued. Berkeley: Blue Wind Press, 1980.

Bibliography

Lee Harwood

Title Illegible. London: Writers Forum, 1965.
The Man With Blue Eyes. New York: Angel Hair Books, 1966.
The White Room. London: Fulcrum Press, 1968. Includes *Title Illegible*, *The Man With Blue Eyes*, and other poetry.
The Beautiful Atlas. Brighton: Ted Kavanagh, 1969.
Landscapes. London: Fulcrum Press, 1969.
The Sinking Colony. London: Fulcrum Press, 1970.
The First Poem. Brighton: Unicorn Bookshop, 1971.
New Year. London: Larry & Ruby Wallrich, 1971.
Captain Harwood's Log of Stern Statements and Stout Sayings. London: Writers Forum, 1973.
Freighters: From Notes of a Post Office Clerk. Newcastle upon Tyne: Pig Press, 1975.
HMS Little Fox. London: Oasis Books, 1976.
Old Bosham Bird Watch and Other Stories. Newcastle upon Tyne: Pig Press, 1977; revised, 1978.
Boston-Brighton. London: Oasis Books, 1977.
Wish You Were Here (with Antony Lopez). Deal, Kent: Transgravity Press, 1979.
All the Wrong Notes. Durham: Pig Press, 1981.

Tom Raworth

Weapon-Man. London: Goliard Press, 1965.
Continuation: Poem. London: Goliard Press, 1966.
The Relation Ship: Poems. London: Goliard Press, 1967; New York: Grossman Publishers, 1969.
Haiku (with John Esam and Anselm Hollo). London: Trigram Press, 1968.
The Big Green Day. London: Trigram Press, 1968.
A Serial Biography. London: Fulcrum Press, 1969.
Lion, Lion. London: Trigram Press, 1970.
Moving. London: Cape Goliard, 1971; New York: Grossman Publishers, 1971.
Pleasant Butter. Northampton, Mass.: Sand Project Press, 1972.
Tracking. Bowling Green, Ohio: Doones Press, 1972.
Time Being (with Asa Benveniste and Ray DiPalma). London: Blue Chair, 1972.
Back to Nature. London: Joe DiMaggio Press, 1973.
Act. London: Trigram Press, 1973.
The Auction of Olson's Head. Chicago: Ommation Press, 1977.
Bolivia: Another End of Ace. London: Secret Books, 1974.

Bibliography

Ace. London: Cape Goliard, 1974; Berkeley: Figures Press, 1977.

Cloister. Northampton, Mass.: Sand Project Press, 1975.

The More Simple Natural Time Tone Distortion. Storrs, Conn.: University of Connecticut Library, 1975.

Energy Gap. Chicago: Ommation Press, 1976.

The Mask. Berkeley: Poltroon Press, 1976.

Sky Tails. Cambridge: Lobby Press, 1978.

Four Door Guide. Cambridge: Street Editions, 1979.

Writing. Durham, N.C.: Bull City Press, 1979.

Heavy Light. Colchester, Essex: Transgravity Press, 1979.

Nicht Wahr, Rosie? Berkeley: Poltroon Press, 1979.

Index

233

Index

Index

Acknowledgments

Grateful acknowledgment is made to those named below for permission to quote from the works listed:

From *The Necklace* (1955), *Seeing Is Believing* (1958), *A Peopled Landscape* (1963), *American Scenes and Other Poems* (1966), *The Way of a World* (1969), *Written on Water* (1972), *The Way In and Other Poems* (1974), and *The Shaft* (1978), by Charles Tomlinson, reprinted by permission of Oxford University Press.

From *Identities and Other Poems* (1964, 1967), by Matthew Mead, by permission of Matthew Mead; from *The Administration of Things* (1970), by Matthew Mead, and Sabais's *Generation and Other Poems*, translated by Matthew Mead, by permission of Anvil Press Poetry Ltd.

From *For the Unfallen: Poems 1952–1958* (1959), *King Log* (1968), *Mercian Hymns* (1971), and *Tenebrae* (1978), by Geoffrey Hill, by permission of Andre Deutsch Ltd.; from *Somewhere Is Such a Kingdom*, by Geoffrey Hill. Copyright © 1975 by Geoffrey Hill. Reprinted by permission of Houghton Mifflin Company; from *Tenebrae*, by Geoffrey Hill. Copyright © 1978 by Geoffrey Hill. Reprinted by permission of Houghton Mifflin Company.

From *The Hawk in the Rain* (1957), *Lupercal* (1960), *Wodwo* (1967), *Crow: From the Life and Songs of the Crow* (1970), *Season Songs* (1976), *Gaudete* (1977), *Cave Birds* (1978), *Moortown* (1979), and *Under the North Star* (1981), by Ted Hughes, reprinted by permission of Faber and Faber Ltd. From *The Hawk in the Rain, Lupercal, Wodwo, Crow, Season Songs, Under the North Star,* and *New Selected Poems* (1982), by Ted Hughes, reprinted by permission from Harper & Row, Publishers, Inc. From *Cave Birds*, by Ted Hughes, reprinted by permission of Viking Penguin, Inc. From *Selected Poems of Vasko Popa*, trans. Anne Pennington, reprinted by permission of Peter Jay.

From *In Parenthesis* (1937), *The Anathémata* (1952), and *The Sleeping Lord* (1974), by David Jones, reprinted by permission of Faber and Faber Ltd. and Nathaniel Hoffman.

From *Collected Poems* (1978), by Basil Bunting, by permission of Oxford University Press.

From *& It Is a Song* (1965) and *Faces & Forms* (1965), by Anselm Hollo, reprinted by permission of Ambit Press; from *The Man in the Treetop Hat* (1968), *The Coherences* (1968), and *Alembic* (1972), by Anselm Hollo, reprinted by permission, © Anselm Hollo, 1982; from *Maya* (1970), by Anselm Hollo, reprinted by permission of Cape Goliard Press.

Acknowledgments

From *The White Room* (1968), *Landscapes* (1969), *The Sinking Colony* (1970), *Freighters* (1975), *HMS Little Fox* (1976), and *Old Bosham Bird Watch and Other Stories* (1977), by Lee Harwood, texts copyright © Lee Harwood, reprinted by permission.

From *The Relation Ship* (1967), *The Big Green Day* (1968), *Moving* (1971), and *Act* (1973), by Tom Raworth, reprinted by permission of Tom Raworth.

Permission from the *Iowa Review* to reprint parts of my essays "Charles Tomlinson: With Respect to Flux" and "Geoffrey Hill" (*Iowa Review* Fall 1976 and Fall 1977); and from the University of Texas Press to reprint parts of my essay "Ted Hughes, *Crow*, and Pain" (*Texas Quarterly* 1976) is gratefully acknowledged.

In addition, I acknowledge with gratitude receipt of a Senior Fellowship from the National Endowment for the Humanities and a sabbatical leave from the University of Oregon that enabled me to spend an academic year reading contemporary British poetry. For hospitality in Keynes College, Canterbury, during that year I thank the Master, Derek Crabtree. I am grateful to the American Council of Learned Societies for a Grant-in-Aid for further pursuit of these studies; to Robert J. Bertholf, Roy Fisher, Matthew Mead, Eric Mottram, Charles Tomlinson, Ingrid Weatherhead, and George Wickes, for conversations and correspondence on this subject. I am indebted to J. Richard Heinzkill of the University of Oregon Library for making the bibliography; to Jonathan Barker for assistance in the Arts Council Library in London; and to Dean Robert M. Berdahl, Jeanine Jenks, and Andrea Weatherhead, for miscellaneous assistance.

A. K. W.
Eugene, Oregon
December 1982